1000 FACTS ABOUT THE OLYMPIC GAMES

Content

"The most important thing is not winning but taking part"

— Pierre de Coubertin

Introduction

The Olympic Games: a grand spectacle that binds nations, cultures, and the spirit of competition into a harmonious dance that plays out every four years. It's a symphony of human will, athleticism, and dreams where athletes from the farthest corners of the world gather, showcasing their prowess and representing their countries with pride and passion.

However, behind every leap, throw, sprint, and stroke lies a myriad of stories – tales of resilience, historical quirks, astonishing records, and inspiring feats. This book, "1000 Facts about the Olympic Games", aims to shine a light on these often overlooked facets of the Games. While the spectacle itself is universally acknowledged, many gems remain hidden in the vast chronicles of the Olympics' storied past.

From the sandy arenas of Ancient Greece to the state-of-the-art stadiums of Tokyo, the Olympics have evolved, adapted, and grown, yet have consistently symbolized the unyielding human spirit. Through this compilation, readers will embark on a journey, diving deep into the facts that have shaped the Games into the monumental event it is today.

Whether you're an avid sports enthusiast, a curious historian, or simply a lover of remarkable tales, this book promises a treasure trove of information that will amuse, surprise, and inspire. It's not just about the numbers or records; it's about the heartbeats, the sweat, and the soul of the Olympic Games.

Welcome to a world where every page turn reveals a new facet of the grandest stage in sports. Dive in, explore, and revel in the magic of the Olympic Games.

Daniel Scott

Alpine Skiing

- **Introduction** : Alpine skiing, commonly referred to as downhill skiing, has been part of the Winter Olympics since 1936. It showcases the skills of skiers as they navigate a downhill course set with a variety of gates.
- **Evolutions** : The initial Olympic alpine skiing competitions included only the combined event, with downhill and slalom added in 1948. This evolution showcases the sport's growth and diversification over the years.
- **Record Speed** : Johann Clarey of France reached an astonishing speed of 100.6 mph during the 2013 Lauberhorn World Cup Downhill. This isn't an Olympic event, but it gives an idea of the extreme speeds athletes can achieve in this discipline.
- **Equipment** : In the early 20th century, alpine skiers used wooden skis and simple leather boots. Modern alpine skiing equipment, including advanced carbon-fiber skis and sophisticated boot systems, has revolutionized the sport's dynamics.
- **Gender Milestone** : Women made their alpine skiing Olympic debut in 1948 at the St. Moritz Games. It marked an essential step towards gender equality in winter sports.
- **Comeback** : After breaking her arm and leg in a 2016 crash, Lindsey Vonn made a triumphant return to win a bronze medal in the 2018 PyeongChang Olympics. Her resilience showcases the dedication and passion athletes bring to the sport.
- **Youngest Champion** : At just 20 years old, American skier Mikaela Shiffrin won gold in the slalom at the 2014 Sochi Olympics. Her achievement emphasizes the sport's need for agility, precision, and young talent.
- **Oldest Winner** : Mario Matt of Austria won the men's slalom at 34 years old during the 2014 Sochi Olympics, making him the oldest alpine skiing gold medalist.

- **Safety** : Helmets weren't always mandatory in alpine skiing. Following a series of high-profile accidents, they became compulsory in the 2010s, underlining the sport's commitment to athlete safety.
- **Altitude Impact** : The highest elevation for an alpine skiing race in Olympic history was 2,850 meters, at the 1960 Squaw Valley Olympics. At such altitudes, skiers face challenges like reduced oxygen and varying snow conditions.
- **Tight Margins** : At the 2014 Sochi Olympics, a mere 0.06 seconds separated gold and silver medalists in the men's super-G, illustrating the razor-thin margins in alpine racing.
- **Disciplines** : There are five alpine skiing disciplines at the Olympics: downhill, super-G, giant slalom, slalom, and combined. Each has unique challenges, emphasizing different aspects of the sport.
- **Snow Control** : Man-made snow is sometimes used in the Olympics if natural conditions are insufficient. For instance, the 1988 Calgary Olympics utilized snow-making machines to ensure optimal race conditions.
- **Twin Success** : Identical twin brothers Phil and Steve Mahre won gold and silver respectively in the men's slalom at the 1984 Sarajevo Olympics, a testament to their shared talent and dedication.
- **Course Complexity** : An Olympic downhill course can have a vertical drop of up to 1,100 meters. This descent tests athletes' stamina, speed, and technique over diverse terrains.
- **Weather Challenges** : The 1998 Nagano Olympics saw heavy rain and fog affecting the men's downhill event, proving that unpredictable weather is a formidable opponent in alpine skiing.
- **Double Duty** : Erika Hess of Switzerland is one of the few skiers to win two individual gold medals (in slalom and giant slalom) during a single Olympics, achieving this feat in 1984.
- **Spectator Impact** : At the 2018 PyeongChang Olympics, over 55,000 spectators watched the men's downhill race, highlighting

the sport's immense popularity and the exhilarating experience it offers to viewers.

- **Ski Length** : While early Olympic skiers used skis that were much taller than them, today's regulations for men's slalom demand skis be at least 165 cm in length. This shift prioritizes agility and responsiveness.
- **Pioneering Nations** : France, Austria, and Switzerland are among the top-performing countries in alpine skiing, having collectively earned over 100 Olympic medals by 2018. Their alpine regions and rich skiing traditions have fostered world-class talent.

Archery

- **Revival** : Archery was introduced to the Olympic Games in 1900. However, due to inconsistencies in rules, it was discontinued in 1920 and reintroduced in 1972 with standardized global rules.
- **Gender Inclusivity** : Women were allowed to compete in Olympic archery from its inception. This made the 1904 St. Louis Games the first to feature female competitors in any sport.
- **Marathon Match** : In the 1920 Olympics, the men's double York round had archers shoot an incredible 144 arrows. This grueling format tested both stamina and precision over hours of competition.
- **Korean Dominance** : South Korea's archery team has been exceptional, winning 23 out of 34 possible gold medals between 1984 and 2016. Their disciplined training regimen has set a gold standard in the sport.
- **Youngest Winner** : Kim Yun-Mi of South Korea won a gold medal in archery at just 17 years of age during the 1992 Barcelona Olympics. Her victory showcased that age is no barrier to excellence.

- **Distance Precision** : Archers at the Olympics shoot at targets 70 meters away. To visualize this, it's like aiming at an apple from the length of a football field.
- **Perfect Score** : South Korean archer Im Dong-Hyun, legally blind in one eye, set a world record in 2012 by scoring 699 out of a possible 720 points. His accomplishment underlines the importance of skill over perfect vision in the sport.
- **Consecutive Wins** : South Korean archer Kim Soo-Nyung won medals at four consecutive Olympics from 1988 to 2000. Her consistent performance over a long period is a testament to her enduring talent.
- **Outdoor to Indoor** : While modern Olympic archery events are held outdoors, the 1900 Paris Games had competitions inside the Bois de Vincennes. It's a striking contrast to today's wind and weather-influenced matches.
- **Team Synergy** : Team archery was introduced to the Olympics in 1988. It requires three archers per nation to synchronize their skills for collective success.
- **Sudden Death** : In case of a tie, a one-arrow shoot-off determines the winner. This intense decider amplifies the pressure and excitement for both competitors and spectators.
- **Consistent Venue** : Since its reintroduction in 1972, all Olympic archery events have been held at the same location as the Opening Ceremony, giving the sport a prestigious platform.
- **Bow Evolution** : Early Olympic archers used wooden longbows. Today's competitors use sophisticated recurve bows, highlighting the sport's technological evolution.
- **Amid Ruins** : The 2004 Athens Olympics had archers compete in the Panathenaic Stadium, a venue dating back to 330 BC. The blend of ancient history and modern sport was truly breathtaking.
- **Record Audience** : Over 65,000 spectators watched the archery finals at the 2012 London Olympics. The iconic Lord's Cricket Ground venue enhanced the spectacle.

- **Uniform Flair** : At the 2012 London Olympics, the South Korean women's team wore hats to protect against rain, leading to a trend in fashionable archery headgear.
- **Family Ties** : In the 1988 Seoul Olympics, siblings Tomi and Petra Ericsson represented Finland in archery. Such familial partnerships underline the sport's deep-rooted traditions.
- **Hometown Advantage** : The US men's team won gold when archery made its Olympic debut in 1900 in Paris. Host nation advantages were evident even a century ago!
- **All-Rounder** : Hubert Van Innis of Belgium remains the most decorated Olympic archer, securing 9 medals (6 gold, 3 silver) in 1900 and 1920. His versatility across various formats was unmatched.
- **Underdogs** : Despite not being a traditional powerhouse, Indonesia secured its first Olympic gold in 2020 in mixed team archery. Such surprises are what make the Olympic archery competitions so unpredictable and exciting.

Athletic Walking

- **Origins** : Race walking, often referred to as athletic walking, has its roots in competitive long-distance walking events in Britain. It made its Olympic debut in 1904, showcasing a unique blend of endurance and technique.
- **Distinctive Rule** : The key rule differentiating race walking from running is that one foot must always be in contact with the ground. This demands immense discipline and technique from athletes.
- **Men's Distance** : Men's race walking in the Olympics originally had varying distances. It wasn't until 1956 that the 20km and 50km became standardized distances for male competitors.
- **Women's Inclusion** : Women were only allowed to compete in the Olympic race walking event from 1992. It marked a significant step towards gender equality in this discipline.

- **Endurance Test** : The 50km race walking event is the longest athletic event in the Olympics. Completing it is a testament to an athlete's stamina, resilience, and technique.
- **Speed** : Yohann Diniz of France holds the 50km race walk world record, completing it in 3 hours, 32 minutes, and 33 seconds in 2014. It's an astonishing pace, averaging under 4.25 minutes per kilometer.
- **Venue Shift** : Originally, race walking took place on a stadium track. From 1956, events were held on public roads, reflecting the discipline's long-distance roots.
- **Double Victory** : In 1984, Italian athlete Maurizio Damilano became the first and only man to win both the 20km and 50km World Championships in race walking. A truly remarkable feat in two such grueling events.
- **Young Achiever** : At 22 years, Ecuador's Jefferson Pérez won the 20km race walk at the 1996 Atlanta Olympics. He remains the youngest gold medalist in this event's history.
- **Legendary Streak** : Between 1960 and 1976, the Soviet Union won the men's 20km race walking event in four consecutive Olympics, underscoring their dominance in the discipline.
- **Stalwart** : Jesus Angel Garcia of Spain has the record for the most World Championships appearances in race walking, with a whopping 13 participations between 1991 and 2019.
- **Heartbreak** : In the 2016 Rio Olympics, Hirooki Arai of Japan initially finished third in the 50km race walk but was disqualified. However, upon appeal, he was reinstated and awarded his bronze medal.
- **High Participation** : The 20km race walk at the 2012 London Olympics saw 56 competitors, the highest in Olympic history for this event.
- **Altitude Impact** : The 1968 Mexico City Olympics posed a unique challenge as race walkers had to compete at 2,250 meters above sea level. The thin air tested the athletes' adaptability and endurance to the limits.

- **Form and Function** : Judges are stationed along the race walking route to ensure athletes maintain proper form. Three warnings from different judges lead to disqualification, emphasizing the importance of technique.
- **Unpredictability** : Despite the sport's paced nature, lead changes are common in race walking, making it an exciting event for spectators as favorites can be overtaken.
- **Epic Battles** : The 2000 Sydney Olympics saw a fierce competition between Robert Korzeniowski of Poland and Aigars Fadejevs of Latvia in the 50km event, with Korzeniowski triumphing by just 17 seconds.
- **Spotless Win** : In 2012, Elena Lashmanova of Russia set a world record in the women's 20km race walk at the London Olympics, finishing in 1 hour, 25 minutes, and 2 seconds without receiving a single warning.
- **Evolving Techniques** : Over decades, race walkers have modified their techniques, including arm movement and stride, to gain speed while staying within rules. This evolution reflects the sport's continuous quest for optimization.
- **Global Spread** : Despite Europe's dominance, countries like China, Mexico, and Australia have produced top race walkers in recent years, highlighting the sport's global appeal and reach.

Badminton

- **Debut** : Badminton made its Olympic debut relatively recently in 1992 in Barcelona. Since then, it has become an integral part of the Summer Games, attracting a global audience.
- **Dominance** : Asian countries, particularly China, Indonesia, and South Korea, have historically dominated Olympic badminton. Together, they've won a staggering 93 out of the 106 medals awarded until 2021.

- **Sweep** : At the 2012 London Olympics, China astonishingly claimed all five gold medals in badminton across singles and doubles categories.
- **Shuttle Speed** : When Fu Haifeng of China hit a shuttlecock in 2005, he set a world record speed of 332 km/h (206 mph). Though it wasn't during the Olympics, this fact showcases the intensity of elite badminton.
- **Lengthy Marathon** : The longest match in Olympic badminton history was a 124-minute men's doubles match in the 2000 Sydney Olympics. It was a true test of stamina and resilience.
- **Young Achiever** : At just 16 years of age, Gu Jinhua became the youngest badminton player to win an Olympic medal, clinching gold in women's doubles at the 1992 Barcelona Games.
- **Format Shift** : The original Olympic badminton format was a knockout system. However, in 2012, a group stage followed by a knockout phase was introduced, offering players more matches and chances.
- **Scoring Evolution** : The scoring system evolved to a rally-point system in 2006, where points can be scored by the server or the receiver. This change made Olympic matches faster and more unpredictable.
- **Team Exclusion** : In a shocking twist during the 2012 London Olympics, eight female players from South Korea, China, and Indonesia were disqualified for "not using one's best efforts to win" after allegedly throwing their matches to secure favorable draws.
- **Venue Acoustics** : The acoustics of a badminton venue play a significant role. At the 2008 Beijing Olympics, players complained about not hearing the shuttle due to the noise, demonstrating the importance of venue design.
- **Feathered Affair** : Olympic badminton shuttlecocks are made of feathers, often from ducks or geese. Approximately 16 feathers are used for one shuttlecock, showcasing the meticulous nature of the sport's equipment.

- **Recurring Champions** : Only three badminton players have ever successfully defended their singles titles at the Olympics - Lin Dan for men (2008 and 2012) and Zhang Ning (2004 and 2008) & Carolina Marin (2016 and 2020) for women.
- **Racket Tech** : Over the decades, rackets have evolved from wooden to lightweight carbon-fiber composites. The 1996 Atlanta Games was one of the first to showcase these advanced rackets.
- **Maximum Nations** : The 1996 Atlanta Olympics saw a record 37 nations competing in badminton, underscoring the sport's global appeal.
- **Danish Exception** : Denmark's Poul-Erik Høyer Larsen's victory in men's singles at the 1996 Atlanta Olympics stands out. He's the only European male badminton player to have won Olympic gold in this event.
- **Singles Sweep** : Since badminton's Olympic inclusion in 1992, only China has managed to win both men's and women's singles gold at the same Olympics - a feat they achieved twice (2008 and 2012).
- **Uniform Change** : The 2012 Olympics marked a change where women players were allowed to wear shorts or skirts, adding flexibility to their choices and showcasing evolving sports fashion standards.
- **Left-handers' Might** : Left-handed players like Lin Dan and Carolina Marin have often been at the forefront of Olympic badminton, suggesting a unique advantage or style they bring to the court.
- **Duration Diversity** : While badminton matches can be swift, there's a significant range in duration. At the 2016 Rio Olympics, matches ranged from just 19 minutes to a marathon 92 minutes.
- **Spectators' Love** : Badminton is among the most-watched sports in the Olympics. The 2012 London Games had over 1.4 billion viewers for badminton, emphasizing its immense global appeal.

Basketball

- **Inception** : Basketball was introduced to the Olympics in 1936 during the Berlin Games. Interestingly, the sport was played outdoors on a clay and sand court, which affected the game dynamics.
- **Female Representation** : Women's basketball had to wait until 1976 in Montreal to make its Olympic debut. This inclusion marked a significant stride towards gender equality in the Games.
- **American Dominance** : The USA Men's Basketball team has secured gold a whopping 15 times out of the 19 Olympics they participated in till 2021, underlining their dominance in the sport.
- **Undefeated Streak** : The USA Women's Basketball team has an incredible streak, winning gold consecutively from 1996 to 2021, showcasing their unparalleled skill and teamwork.
- **Tallest Olympian** : At 7 feet 6 inches, Yao Ming of China, who played in the 2000, 2004, and 2008 Olympics, is one of the tallest Olympic basketball players ever, making him a formidable presence on the court.
- **Dream Team** : The 1992 Barcelona Olympics introduced NBA players to the Games. The US team, famously known as the "Dream Team", had legends like Michael Jordan, Magic Johnson, and Larry Bird.
- **Closest Finish** : In 1972, the Soviet Union controversially beat the USA by one point (51-50) in a match that remains one of the most debated in Olympic history due to its contentious ending.
- **Four Decades** : Brazilian legend Oscar Schmidt played in five Olympics, from 1980 to 1996, amassing an awe-inspiring total of 1,093 points throughout his Olympic career.
- **Olympic Scoring Record** : Lisa Leslie of the USA scored 35 points in a game during the 2006 Athens Olympics, a record for a women's Olympic basketball match.
- **Triple Participations** : The 2021 Tokyo Olympics saw three NBA players—Luka Dončić, Patty Mills, and Kevin Durant—score 50 or

more points in a single game, a testament to the elevated skill level of the competition.

- **Venue Variations** : Unlike the initial 1936 Games, all basketball matches post-1972 have been played indoors, enhancing the viewing experience and game quality.
- **Argentine Surprise** : In 2004, Argentina's men's team stunned everyone by winning gold, breaking the USA's streak and proving the sport's unpredictable nature.
- **Female Pioneers** : The Unified Team, representing several republics of the former Soviet Union, won the inaugural women's basketball gold in 1992.
- **Spanish Consistency** : As of 2021, Spain's men's basketball team has secured medals in three of the last five Olympics, emphasizing their consistent performance on the global stage.
- **Age Record** : Sue Bird and Diana Taurasi, both from the USA, competed in their fifth Olympics in 2021, tying Teresa Edwards' record for basketball participation.
- **Twin Gold** : In 2012, the USA became the first country to win gold in both men's and women's basketball at the same Olympics since the USSR in 1988.
- **Unprecedented Growth** : Since its introduction in 1936, the number of nations competing in basketball has risen from 21 to 30 by the 2021 Tokyo Olympics.
- **Dynamic Duo** : Anne Donovan and Lisa Leslie are the only two players to win gold as both a player and a coach in the Olympics, showcasing their multifaceted contributions to the game.
- **Double Digits** : The 1996 US Women's basketball team won their matches by an average margin of 28.8 points, proving their dominant performance throughout the campaign.
- **Versatility Showcased** : 3x3 basketball made its debut in the 2021 Tokyo Olympics, providing a faster-paced and unique version of the traditional game, emphasizing the sport's adaptability and evolution.

Biathlon

- **Origins** : Biathlon stems from the ancient hunting practices of northern Europe. Initially, it involved skiing in the mountains and forests while hunting game.
- **Olympic Introduction** : Biathlon, as a military patrol, was a demonstration sport in the 1924 Chamonix Games. It wasn't until 1960 in Squaw Valley that it was added as a competitive sport.
- **Women's Debut** : Women's biathlon events were included much later, with their Olympic debut happening in the 1992 Albertville Games.
- **Norwegian Dominance** : Ole Einar Bjørndalen of Norway, often termed as the "King of Biathlon", has won 13 Olympic medals (8 golds), making him the most decorated biathlete in Olympic history.
- **Perfect Score** : Achieving a perfect shooting score in the Olympics is rare due to the intense pressure. However, Raphaël Poirée did so in the 2002 Salt Lake City Olympics, impressing everyone.
- **Twist of Fate** : During the 1968 Grenoble Olympics, Sweden's Lars-Göran Arwidson shot flawlessly but still finished second. The winner, Magnar Solberg of Norway, missed a target but had a superior skiing time.
- **Family Ties** : The Fourcade siblings from France have both made their mark in Olympic biathlon. Martin Fourcade has won five gold medals, while his sister, Marie Dorin Habert, has also clinched an Olympic medal.
- **Changing Formats** : Biathlon at the Olympics initially consisted of only individual men's 20 km. Now, it has grown to include sprint, pursuit, relay, and mass start races for both men and women.
- **Diverse Champions** : As of 2021, Norway, Germany, Russia, and France are the only countries to have won more than ten Olympic

gold medals in biathlon, showcasing the sport's competitive nature.

- **Unpredictable Results** : In the 2018 Pyeongchang Olympics, Sweden's Hanna Öberg surprised many by winning gold in the women's 15 km individual, even though it was her Olympic debut.
- **Age No Bar** : Norway's Halvard Hanevold proved that age is just a number when he won a relay gold at the 2010 Vancouver Olympics at the ripe age of 40.
- **Multiple Disciplines** : Only three biathletes have ever won gold medals in three different types of biathlon events in a single Olympics, with Ole Einar Bjørndalen being one of them in 2002.
- **Target Dynamics** : From 1960 to 1979, targets were 150mm in diameter. They were reduced to 115mm for individual and sprint events from 1980 onwards to increase the challenge.
- **Unbeatable Streak** : Germany's women's relay team won gold in three consecutive Olympics from 1998 to 2006, showcasing an unmatched streak of dominance.
- **Shoot to Win** : In biathlon, each missed shot results in a one-minute penalty in individual races or a 150m penalty lap in other formats. This has led to dramatic shifts in podium finishes at the Olympics.
- **Altitude Impact** : The 1968 Grenoble Olympics posed a unique challenge as the biathlon events were held at an altitude of 1,800 meters, testing athletes' endurance more than usual.
- **Zeroing in** : Before each race, biathletes are given a "zeroing" period to calibrate their rifles, a crucial aspect for their shooting accuracy during the actual event.
- **Unique Shooting** : Unlike many shooting sports, in biathlon, athletes shoot in two positions – prone and standing, making it doubly challenging, especially after intense skiing sessions.
- **Defying Expectations** : Despite being a powerhouse, Germany's Men's team had to wait until 2006 to win their first relay gold in the Olympics, proving the unpredictability of the sport.

- **Mass Start Drama** : Introduced in the 2006 Turin Games, the mass start event where all biathletes start simultaneously has since been a thrilling addition, often leading to nail-biting finishes.

Bobsleigh

- **Inception** : The sport of bobsleigh began in Switzerland in the late 19th century. By 1924, it had made its Olympic debut at the Winter Games in Chamonix.
- **Monobob** : Women's monobob made its Olympic debut in 2022 at the Beijing Winter Games. Unlike traditional formats, it features just one athlete, emphasizing individual skill and prowess.
- **No Brakes** : Bobsleds can reach speeds of over 150 km/h (93 mph). The unique thing? They don't have any brakes until they cross the finish line.
- **Eugenio Monti's Sportsmanship** : During the 1964 Innsbruck Olympics, Italian Eugenio Monti offered a critical part of his own bobsled to the British team, who then went on to win gold, showcasing unparalleled sportsmanship.
- **Jamaican Surprise** : The 1988 Calgary Winter Olympics saw Jamaica's debut in bobsleigh. The tropical nation's unexpected participation inspired the popular movie "Cool Runnings."
- **Weighty Matters** : The maximum weight, including the crew, for a two-man bobsled is 390 kg, ensuring that strength and speed, not just weight, determine the sled's pace.
- **Safety First** : Following a tragic accident in the 1964 Innsbruck Games, bobsleigh tracks underwent a redesign. The changes made the tracks more technical and less dangerous.
- **Golden Streak** : Between 1964 and 2002, the German men's teams won eight gold medals in the four-man event, demonstrating incredible consistency.

- **Unbeaten Record** : At the 2010 Vancouver Olympics, Canada's team set an unbeatable Whistler Sliding Centre track record of 50.86 seconds in the two-man event.
- **Natural to Artificial** : Originally, bobsleigh tracks were carved from natural ice. The 1960 Squaw Valley Winter Olympics was the last to use such a track before the transition to artificially refrigerated tracks.
- **US Women's Triumph** : The USA Women's bobsleigh team clinched their first-ever gold in the event at the 2002 Salt Lake City Olympics, ending a long-awaited chase for the top podium spot.
- **Reinstated** : Women's bobsleigh, after a prolonged hiatus, was reintroduced in the 2002 Olympics, encouraging gender parity in the sport.
- **High G-Force** : Athletes experience forces up to 5G during turns, equivalent to some of the most extreme roller coasters in the world.
- **Oldest Winner** : At 40 years and 5 days old, André Lange of Germany became the oldest pilot to win an Olympic gold in bobsleigh during the 2010 Vancouver Games.
- **Discontinued Format** : A four-woman bobsleigh event was planned for the 1940 Olympics (which were canceled). This format hasn't yet been revisited in the Olympic Games.
- **Underdog Win** : At the 2018 Pyeongchang Olympics, the German team of Francesco Friedrich tied with the Canadian team for gold in the two-man bobsleigh, marking a rare tie in the event's history.
- **Crucial Start** : The first 50 meters of a bobsleigh run, known as the start, can make or break a race. Pushing the sled powerfully and quickly hopping in can determine the sled's speed throughout the race.
- **Resilient Return** : After a 62-year absence, the Indian bobsleigh team made a comeback in the 2018 Pyeongchang Winter Olympics, showcasing resilience and passion for the sport.

- **Origin of Name** : The term "bobsleigh" derives from early racers bobbing back and forth to increase speed. Though the technique changed, the name remained.
- **Evolving Design** : In the 1950s and 1960s, the Italian-made Ferrari bobsleds dominated the sport. Today, sleds have evolved with aerodynamics and technological advancements to be faster and more efficient.

Boxing

- **Ancient Roots** : Boxing has a rich history, dating back to the ancient Greeks. It made its Olympic debut in 688 B.C. at the 23rd Olympiad.
- **Modern Return** : After being absent for centuries, boxing re-entered the Olympic scene in 1904 at the St. Louis Games, marking a revival of the ancient tradition.
- **First Champions** : The 1904 Olympics saw only American boxers competing. This ensured a clean sweep for the United States in all boxing categories.
- **Women's Inclusion** : Women's boxing was notably absent from the Olympics until recently. The 2012 London Games witnessed the inaugural women's boxing competitions.
- **Biting Incident** : In 1988, during a match in Seoul, New Zealand boxer Kevin Barry's opponent bit him. The bizarre act resulted in the opponent's disqualification, awarding Barry a bronze medal.
- **Pro Move** : Historically, professional boxers couldn't compete in the Olympics. This changed in 2016 when pros were allowed to qualify for the Rio Games.
- **Cassius Clay** : The iconic Muhammad Ali, then Cassius Clay, first gained international acclaim by winning a gold medal at the 1960 Rome Olympics in the light heavyweight division.
- **Five-time Champ** : Teófilo Stevenson of Cuba is a boxing legend with three Olympic gold medals. However, had Cuba not

boycotted the 1980 and 1984 Games, Stevenson might have clinched five.

- **Referee's Call** : In boxing, the referee can stop a bout if one competitor receives more than 20 blows to the head in one round. Safety always comes first.
- **No Headgear** : The 2016 Rio de Janeiro Games witnessed male boxers competing without headgear, a significant change from previous Olympic events.
- **Boxing Siblings** : Aldo and Nino Spoldi from Italy became the first brothers to compete in Olympic boxing, showcasing their skills in the 1924 Paris Games.
- **Unique Record** : Filipino boxer Mansueto Velasco clinched silver in the 1996 Atlanta Games. His younger brother, Roel, matched this feat four years later in Sydney, making them the only siblings to win identical Olympic boxing medals.
- **Medal Tally** : As of 2021, the USA holds the record with 50 gold medals in Olympic boxing, reflecting the country's dominant history in the sport.
- **Twin Gold** : At the 1976 Montreal Games, Soviet twins Vladimir and Viktor Alekseev both achieved gold in different weight categories, showcasing their shared boxing prowess.
- **Second Chance** : If a boxer is defeated by the eventual gold medalist, they can compete in a "repechage", providing a route to potentially win bronze.
- **Youngest Winner** : Spain's Baltasar Sangchili, at 17, became the youngest boxer to win Olympic gold when he triumphed in the 1924 Paris Games in the flyweight division.
- **Unified Korea** : In a move towards peace, North and South Korean female boxers united to form a single team during the 2018 Asian Games, highlighting the unifying power of sports.
- **Diverse Finals** : The 2016 Rio Games saw finalists in the boxing event represent a record 23 different nations, emphasizing the sport's global appeal.

- **White Towel** : Originating from boxing's early days, when a boxer's corner throws in a white towel, it signals their wish to forfeit the match. This tradition remains in Olympic boxing.
- **Lightest Category** : The lightest Olympic boxing category is the light flyweight, with boxers weighing up to 49 kg (108 lbs), showcasing agility and speed over sheer power.

Canoe Kayak

- **Debut** : Canoeing made its Olympic entrance in the 1936 Berlin Games. Initially, the event was exclusively for men, showcasing both solo and pair competitions.
- **Kayak Introduction** : While canoeing started in 1936, kayaking events were later introduced. The 1948 London Games included kayaking, expanding the aquatic opportunities for athletes.
- **Gender Equality** : Women first paddled their way into Olympic canoeing in the 1948 London Games, marking a significant step towards gender inclusivity in the sport.
- **Slalom** : Besides sprint racing, the canoe slalom was introduced in the 1972 Munich Games. This event requires paddlers to navigate a whitewater course filled with gates.
- **C-1 and K-1** : The designations "C" and "K" represent canoe and kayak, respectively. The number following indicates the number of paddlers, with "1" being solo and "2" for pairs.
- **Aussie Legend** : Australian kayaker Ian Ferguson is a force to be reckoned with, having won four gold medals across three Olympics (1984, 1988, 1992).
- **Germany's Dominance** : As of 2021, Germany leads the Olympic medal tally for canoe-kayak with over 40 gold medals, showcasing the country's prowess in the water.
- **Canoe Switch** : While most Olympic sports see athletes remaining in their discipline, New Zealand's Ian Ferguson won gold in both canoe and kayak events during the 1984 Los Angeles Games.

- **Versatile Paddle** : In canoes, athletes use single-bladed paddles, while kayakers use double-bladed ones. This distinction leads to different techniques and strategies in races.
- **Endurance Test** : The longest canoe-kayak Olympic race is the 1000m sprint. Athletes require both speed and stamina to excel in this challenging distance.
- **Rapid Addition** : The latest addition to the Olympic canoe-kayak program is the women's C-1 slalom, introduced in the 2020 Tokyo Games.
- **Water Dynamics** : For slalom events, about 15,000 liters of water is pumped every second to replicate a rapid river's dynamic flow, ensuring a challenging course.
- **Polish Achievement** : Polish kayaker, Adam Seroczyński, competed in four consecutive Olympics from 1996 to 2008 and achieved medals in three different kayak categories.
- **Close Finish** : In the 2004 Athens Games, the K-1 500m women's final saw the first four finishers within 0.3 seconds of each other, illustrating the fierce competition.
- **Race Evolution** : Initially, the 10,000m race was part of the Olympic program but was dropped after the 1956 Games. Nowadays, the longest Olympic canoe-kayak race is the 1000m.
- **Gate Importance** : In the slalom event, missing a gate incurs a 50-second penalty. Precision and agility are essential to avoid such hefty time additions.
- **Artificial Course** : The 2020 Tokyo Games showcased canoeing in an artificial slalom course at the Kasai Canoe Slalom Center, designed to challenge the world's best paddlers.
- **Double Gold** : Birgit Fischer of Germany is an eight-time Olympic gold medalist, showcasing her prowess in both kayak singles and doubles across six different Olympic Games.
- **Whitewater Challenge** : The slalom event's courses consist of up to 25 gates, with some requiring upstream navigation, challenging the paddlers' skills and endurance.

- **Craft Design** : Canoes are distinguished by an open cockpit, while kayaks envelop the paddler's legs. This design difference significantly impacts the athletes' seating and paddling positions.

Cross-country skiing

- **Inception** : Cross-country skiing made its Olympic debut during the first Winter Games in Chamonix, 1924. Back then, there were only two events for men, drastically different from today's expanded roster.
- **Women's Debut** : Women didn't compete in Olympic cross-country skiing until the 1952 Oslo Games. Their inclusion was a significant step towards gender equality in winter sports.
- **Marathon Race** : The longest cross-country ski event in the Olympics is the grueling 50km race for men. It requires an astounding blend of stamina and speed.
- **Technique Transition** : In the 1980s, the skating or "freestyle" technique was introduced. By the 1988 Calgary Olympics, separate events for traditional and freestyle techniques were established.
- **Nordic Combined** : This unique event combines cross-country skiing with ski jumping. Athletes compete in both disciplines, and their combined scores determine the winner.
- **Sprint Addition** : The sprint events, covering a mere 1.2-1.6 km, were added to the Olympic program in the 2002 Salt Lake City Games. This addition brought a fast-paced dynamic to the traditionally endurance-focused sport.
- **Pursuit Dynamics** : The pursuit format, introduced in 1992, involves skiers starting in intervals based on previous race times. This system results in a thrilling chase where the first across the finish line wins.

- **Bjørn's Dominance** : Bjørn Dæhlie of Norway won a total of 8 gold medals in cross-country skiing between 1992 and 1998. This achievement remains unmatched in the sport's history.
- **Eero's Legacy** : Eero Mäntyranta, a Finnish skier, boasted a natural mutation that increased his red blood cell count. This advantage helped him secure 3 gold medals between 1960 and 1964.
- **Stance Change** : Traditionally, cross-country skiing had a classic "diagonal stride" technique. However, with the advent of the skating style, athletes could choose between two different skiing techniques in specific events.
- **Team Sprint** : The 2006 Turin Games introduced a new format, the team sprint. Two skiers from each country take turns skiing three laps each, adding a relay dynamic to the sprint.
- **Venue Shift** : For the 2022 Beijing Olympics, cross-country skiing events were held in Zhangjiakou, showcasing the region's ideal snowy conditions.
- **Kalla's Triumph** : Sweden's Charlotte Kalla was the first gold medalist of the 2018 Pyeongchang Olympics, winning the women's 15km skiathlon.
- **Dramatic Finish** : In the 2010 Vancouver Olympics, the women's 10km freestyle had the closest finish ever, with Justyna Kowalczyk beating Sweden's Charlotte Kalla by just 0.3 seconds.
- **Multiple Medals** : In the 2006 Turin Games, Czech skier Kateřina Neumannová managed to secure medals in both individual and team events, showcasing her versatility.
- **Weather Impact** : In the 2018 Pyeongchang Olympics, cross-country ski events faced delays due to strong winds, highlighting the sport's vulnerability to nature's whims.
- **Russian Sweep** : During the 2014 Sochi Olympics, Russia claimed all the podium spots in the men's 50km mass start, marking a historic sweep for the host nation.

- **Equipment Evolution** : Cross-country skis used in the 1924 Chamonix Games were significantly wider and shorter than today's designs, which prioritize speed and maneuverability.
- **Relay Introduction** : The 4x10km relay for men and 4x5km relay for women were added in the 1936 and 1952 Olympics respectively. This addition allowed nations to showcase their depth of talent.
- **Twin Victory** : During the 1960 Squaw Valley Olympics, Finnish twins Juhani and Kalevi Hämäläinen both secured medals in cross-country skiing events, making it a family affair.

Curling

- **Revival** : Curling made its Olympic return at the Nagano 1998 Winter Games after being absent as a medal sport for 74 years. Its reintroduction delighted fans worldwide, showcasing strategic precision on ice.
- **Early Roots** : Curling's Olympic debut was at the inaugural Winter Games in 1924 in Chamonix. However, this participation wasn't officially recognized by the IOC until 2006.
- **Team Composition** : Each curling team, or "rink," comprises four players: a lead, second, third (or vice-skip), and skip. The skip, the strategist, often makes the game-changing decisions.
- **Stone's Journey** : The granite for curling stones predominantly comes from two sources: Ailsa Craig, an island off Scotland, and the Trefor Granite Quarry in Wales, connecting the sport to unique geological landmarks.
- **Swiss Finish** : In the 2002 Salt Lake City Games, Switzerland's women's team clinched the gold medal after a nail-biting extra end, emphasizing the sport's unpredictable nature.
- **Canadian Dominance** : Canada has won three consecutive gold medals in men's curling from 2006 to 2014. This streak underscores the nation's prominence in the sport.

- **Sibling Success** : During the 2014 Sochi Games, British curlers and siblings Anna and Thomas Muirhead both represented their country, marking a family achievement on the Olympic stage.
- **Mixed Doubles** : The 2018 Pyeongchang Winter Olympics introduced mixed doubles curling, adding a fresh dynamic with teams of just two players — one man and one woman.
- **Roaring Game** : Curling is sometimes called the "Roaring Game" because of the sound the stone makes when sliding across pebbled ice. This distinctive noise adds to the sport's unique ambiance.
- **Wheelchair Debut** : Wheelchair curling made its Olympic appearance in the 2006 Turin Paralympics. This inclusion broadened the sport's reach, celebrating athletes' resilience and skill.
- **Determined Comeback** : At the 2018 Pyeongchang Games, the American men's team won their first-ever gold after defeating Sweden, despite starting the tournament with multiple losses.
- **All-Sweep Finish** : In the 2006 Turin Games, Canada achieved a gold medal sweep with both its men's and women's teams standing atop the podium.
- **Measure of Precision** : In curling, an instrument called the "measuring stick" determines which stone is closer to the center. This tool has been crucial in deciding tight matches at the Olympics.
- **Curler's Delivery** : Sliding out of the "hack" to deliver the stone is an art. At the 2010 Vancouver Games, curlers showcased a range of unique delivery styles, from the orthodox to the flamboyant.
- **Swedish Consistency** : Sweden's women's team has secured medals in five consecutive Winter Games from 2002 to 2018, demonstrating their consistency at the highest level.
- **Stone Weight** : The weight of a curling stone used in the Olympics is approximately 42 pounds (19 kg). This standardized weight ensures fairness and consistency in play.

- **Arena Shift** : For the 2022 Beijing Olympics, curling events took place in the Ice Cube Curling Center, a venue specifically designed to accommodate the sport's increasing popularity.
- **Last Stone Advantage** : In the 2018 Pyeongchang final, the U.S. had the "hammer" or last stone advantage in the final end, a strategic edge that played a role in their gold medal victory.
- **Triple Takeout** : In the 2010 Vancouver Olympics, Canadian skip Kevin Martin executed a rare triple takeout, a move where three opposing stones are removed in a single shot, captivating fans worldwide.
- **Youthful Achievement** : In the 2002 Salt Lake City Games, Britain's Rhona Martin, at the age of 36, became one of the sport's older gold medalists, proving that curling is a game of strategy and experience over sheer youth.

Cycling

- **Genesis** : The first Olympic cycling events took place during the inaugural modern Olympic Games in Athens in 1896. Surprisingly, the games featured only track cycling races, introducing audiences to velodrome thrill.
- **Marathon Ride** : The longest Olympic road race was staged in 1912, spanning a staggering 320 kilometers (199 miles). Sweden's Rudolf Lewis clinched the gold after a grueling seven-hour journey.
- **BMX Introduction** : In 2008, the Beijing Olympics introduced BMX racing as an Olympic discipline. This addition emphasized the Olympics' ability to evolve with popular sports trends.
- **Iconic Velodrome** : The London 2012 Olympics showcased the Pringle-shaped Velodrome, an architectural marvel. It became an emblem of the Games and a focal point for track cycling enthusiasts.

- **Women's Debut** : Women's cycling events were first introduced at the 1984 Los Angeles Olympics. This marked a significant step towards gender equality in Olympic sports.
- **Master Climber** : At the 2016 Rio Olympics, Anna van der Breggen from the Netherlands won the women's road race, navigating the grueling climbs to secure gold.
- **Team Pursuit** : The British men's team has secured gold in the team pursuit event in three consecutive Olympics: 2008, 2012, and 2016, showcasing their consistent excellence.
- **Mountain Biking Terrain** : Atlanta's 1996 Olympics were groundbreaking, featuring mountain biking for the first time. Riders braved the rugged Georgia terrains, pushing their limits for Olympic glory.
- **Keirin's Origin** : The Keirin event, a staple in track cycling, has its origins in Japan, dating back to 1948. It was incorporated into the Olympics in 2000, merging tradition with global competition.
- **Back-to-back Victories** : Italy's Paolo Bettini defended his Olympic road race title in 2008 in Beijing, having previously secured gold in Athens 2004. His victories highlighted Italy's enduring cycling prowess.
- **French Dominance** : French cyclists dominated the men's mountain bike event, claiming gold in 1996, 2000, and 2004. This trifecta underlined France's mastery in off-road cycling.
- **Single Day Records** : During the 2012 London Olympics, British cyclists set two world records in a single day in the team pursuit discipline. Their performances left the world in awe.
- **Madison's Return** : The Madison cycling event, which was absent since Beijing 2008, made its anticipated return at the Tokyo 2020 Olympics. Its reintroduction delighted long-time cycling enthusiasts.
- **Solo Endeavor** : The individual time trial, where cyclists race against the clock, was introduced to the Olympics in 1996. It's a true test of endurance and speed over a set distance.

- **Aussie Triumph** : At the 2004 Athens Olympics, Australia's Ryan Bayley won both the individual sprint and the Keirin, emphasizing his sprinting prowess on the track.
- **Medal Sweep** : In the 1908 London Olympics, Great Britain cyclists performed a clean sweep in the 20km track event, securing all the medals on offer.
- **Notable Venue** : The 2004 Athens Olympic velodrome, designed by Santiago Calatrava, became a notable architectural masterpiece, integrating art with sport.
- **German Efficiency** : Kristin Armstrong of the USA and Judith Arndt of Germany both clinched medals in the women's individual time trial in two consecutive Olympics, 2008 and 2012, showcasing their time trial expertise.
- **Dutch Gold** : The Netherlands' Leontien van Moorsel is the only cyclist to have secured gold in both the road race and the individual time trial in a single Olympics, achieving this feat in Sydney 2000.
- **A Unique Quadruple** : Sir Chris Hoy of Great Britain achieved an incredible feat, winning gold medals in four different track cycling events across three Olympics (2004, 2008, and 2012).

Discus Throw

- **Antiquity** : The discus throw can trace its origins back to ancient Greece, around 708 BC. The Olympic Games in ancient times featured this event, marking its enduring legacy in athletics.
- **Modern Debut** : The discus throw was introduced to the modern Olympic Games in 1896 for men. Its popularity ensured it became an Olympic mainstay.
- **Women's Entry** : Women began participating in the discus throw event in the Olympics in 1928. This was a significant step towards inclusion and broadening the event's horizons.
- **Record Distance** : Jürgen Schult of East Germany set an astonishing men's world record in 1986, throwing the discus

74.08 meters. This incredible feat remains unmatched in Olympic history.

- **Soviet Dominance** : The Soviet Union's athletes dominated the women's discus throw, winning every gold medal from 1952 to 1980, emphasizing their sports prowess.
- **Consistent Champion** : Al Oerter of the USA won the discus throw event in four consecutive Olympics from 1956 to 1968. His consistency showcased his elite status in the discipline.
- **Rivalry Story** : The fierce rivalry between Oerter and fellow American Rink Babka during the 1960 Rome Olympics was legendary. Babka led the competition but advised Oerter on his technique, leading to Oerter's gold-winning throw.
- **Youngest Winner** : The youngest gold medalist in discus throw is American Bob Garrett, who was just 20 years old during his 1896 victory in Athens.
- **Ageless Mastery** : At the age of 40, Lia Manoliu of Romania clinched gold in the 1968 Mexico City Olympics, proving age is just a number in this sport.
- **Unique Technique** : Most discus throwers today use the 'rotational technique', which was popularized in the 1950s. However, during the early Olympic Games, athletes utilized a variety of unique throwing techniques.
- **Diverse Podium** : The 2016 Rio Olympics saw athletes from Germany, Poland, and France clinch the top three spots in men's discus throw. It was a celebration of diverse talents from across Europe.
- **Heaviest Discus** : The men's discus weighs 2 kilograms, which might not seem a lot. However, mastering the technique to hurl this weight effectively requires years of rigorous training.
- **Olympic Legend** : Faina Melnik from the Soviet Union set ten world records in discus throw and secured the gold in the 1972 Munich Olympics, making her one of the discipline's legends.

- **Back-to-back Triumphs** : Virgilijus Alekna of Lithuania is one of the few athletes to secure consecutive gold medals in the discus throw, achieving this in 2000 and 2004.
- **Weather Woes** : Weather, especially wind, plays a pivotal role in the discus event. A favorable wind can aid in longer throws, as seen during some record-setting Olympic performances.
- **Venue Icon** : During the 1936 Berlin Olympics, the discus throw was staged at the Maifeld, which could accommodate 120,000 spectators, emphasizing the event's significant following.
- **Family Affair** : Lars Riedel, a five-time World Champion and 1996 Olympic gold medalist, is the son of Hartmut Riedel, another accomplished discus thrower, showcasing their family's deep-rooted talent.
- **Golden Return** : After finishing in the fourth position in 1984, Czechoslovakia's Imrich Bugár made a triumphant return in the 1988 Seoul Olympics, securing a bronze in discus throw.
- **Consistent Podium** : Since the introduction of the women's discus throw event in 1928, no Olympic Games have passed without the event being represented on the podium.
- **Symbolic Value** : The discus throw has often been used as a symbol of the Olympic Games. The iconic image of the discus thrower showcases the grace, strength, and history of the Olympics.

Fencing

- **Ancient Roots** : Fencing has historical roots dating back to ancient Egypt and Greece. However, the sport's modern iteration found its beginnings in Spain during the 15th century.
- **Olympic Inception** : Fencing was one of the original nine sports at the first modern Olympic Games in Athens, 1896, solidifying its place in Olympic heritage.

- **Women's Debut** : Women's fencing made its Olympic debut in 1924, in Paris. This milestone marked another progressive step for gender equality in sports.
- **Three Categories** : Fencing at the Olympics isn't just one event. There are three categories: foil, épée, and sabre, each with distinct rules and techniques.
- **Italian Dominance** : Italy holds the record with a staggering 125 Olympic medals in fencing as of 2021. Their prowess in the sport is unquestioned.
- **Persistent Champion** : Hungarian fencer Aladár Gerevich holds a unique record of winning gold medals in six consecutive Olympics from 1932 to 1960. His consistency is unrivaled in the sport.
- **Team Events** : Team fencing events were introduced to the Olympics in 1904. These events involve strategic bouts between teams from different countries.
- **Diverse Podium** : The 2016 Rio Olympics saw individual épée medals go to Hungary, France, and Korea, showcasing the global appeal and talent in the sport.
- **Olympic Rarity** : Fencing is one of only four sports to have been featured in every modern Olympic Games since its inception in 1896.
- **Wireless Scoring** : The 2004 Athens Olympics introduced wireless electronic scoring for fencing. This technological advance made the sport more dynamic and viewer-friendly.
- **Longest Bout** : The longest Olympic fencing bout took place in 1924, lasting a whopping 1 hour and 37 minutes. The intense duel was eventually won by Italian Oreste Puliti.
- **Sibling Rivalry** : In the 1960 Rome Olympics, brothers Zoltán and Pál Schmitt faced off in the individual sabre event's final, with Zoltán emerging victorious.
- **Mastery Span** : Romanian fencer Ilona Elek won her first Olympic gold in 1936 and then repeated her victory 12 years later in 1948, showcasing her long-spanning dominance.

- **Instantaneous Decisions** : Fencers often have to make decisions in just 1/15th of a second during a bout. This emphasizes the extreme mental alertness required in the sport.
- **Youngest Medalist** : In 1896, Greek fencer Konstantinos Nikolopoulos became the youngest Olympic medalist in fencing at just 14 years old.
- **Oldest Champion** : British fencer Bill Hoskyns won silver in 1960 and 1964, and at the age of 41, he participated in the 1976 Montreal Olympics, showcasing age-defying athleticism.
- **Double-Edged Sword** : While most think of fencing as a purely offensive sport, defense is just as critical. In fact, the term "fencing" is derived from the word "defense."
- **Safety First** : Despite the sport's combative nature, fencing is one of the safest Olympic sports. The tip of the fencing weapon is the second-fastest moving object in any sport, after the marksman's bullet.
- **Historic Venue** : The 1936 Berlin Olympics held the fencing events at the Ruhleben internment camp, a former World War I detention center.
- **Mask Evolution** : Early fencing masks were made of solid black mesh, but after the 1976 Montreal Olympics, transparent masks were introduced, allowing viewers to see fencers' facial expressions.

Figure Skating

- **Historic Debut** : Before the Winter Olympics even existed, figure skating made its Olympic debut in the 1908 Summer Olympics in London. It was the only winter sport to be featured in the Summer Games.
- **Scoring Revolution** : The traditional 6.0 system in figure skating was replaced in 2004 after the Salt Lake City judging controversy. The new International Judging System (IJS) provides a more objective evaluation.

- **Quadruple Frontier** : Canadian skater Kurt Browning made history in 1988 by becoming the first person to land a quadruple jump (four rotations in the air) in competition.
- **Synonymous with Gold** : Sonja Henie of Norway, a legendary figure skater, won three consecutive Olympic golds in 1928, 1932, and 1936, cementing her status as a sport icon.
- **Pair Perfection** : Russians Ekaterina Gordeeva and Sergei Grinkov are one of the few pairs to win two Olympic golds in figure skating (1988 and 1994).
- **Youthful Champion** : American skater Tara Lipinski became the youngest individual gold medalist in Winter Olympic history at 15 years and 255 days during the 1998 Nagano Games.
- **Ballet Crossovers** : John Curry, 1976 gold medalist, is renowned for incorporating ballet and modern dance into his routines, elevating the artistic element of the sport.
- **Innovative Twist** : The first backward outside death spiral was performed by Germans Maxi Herber and Ernst Baier in the 1936 Olympics, a move that's now a pairs' staple.
- **Remarkable Recovery** : Japanese skater Yuzuru Hanyu won the gold in 2018's PyeongChang Olympics just months after sustaining a severe ankle injury.
- **Perfect Sixes** : Oksana Baiul's gold-winning performance in the 1994 Lillehammer Games saw her receiving multiple 6.0s, marking perfection under the old system.
- **Pioneering Pair** : Ludowika and Walter Jakobsson, a married couple, became the first Olympic pairs' champions at the 1920 Summer Olympics in Antwerp.
- **Gender Shift** : Until the 1972 Olympics, male skaters dominated figure skating. However, since then, female skaters have outnumbered their male counterparts in medal counts.
- **Olympic Streak** : Russia (including its previous forms as the Soviet Union) has won gold in the pairs' figure skating event in every Olympics from 1964 to 2006.

- **Synchronized Addition** : Synchronized skating, involving 16 skaters moving as one unit, is seeking inclusion in the Olympics, highlighting the sport's evolving nature.
- **Iconic Costumes** : Peggy Fleming's chartreuse dress from the 1968 Grenoble Olympics remains one of the most iconic figure skating costumes ever, setting trends in fashion-forward sportswear.
- **Triple Axel Achievement** : At the 2018 PyeongChang Olympics, Mirai Nagasu became the first American woman and third overall to land a triple axel in Olympic competition.
- **Rising Age** : While youthful winners were common, the average age of Olympic figure skating champions has increased in recent years, with many in their mid-to-late twenties.
- **Dance Addition** : Ice dancing wasn't introduced to the Olympics until 1976, despite figure skating's earlier Olympic presence.
- **Unconventional Music** : At the PyeongChang 2018 Olympics, skaters could perform to music with lyrics, leading to more diverse and modern song choices.
- **Underdog Triumph** : Sarah Hughes, ranked fourth going into the 2002 Salt Lake City free skate, delivered an impeccable performance, leapfrogging favorites to snatch gold.

Gymnastics

- **Ancient Origins** : Gymnastics was part of the original Olympic Games in ancient Greece, dating back to 776 BC. It was introduced to emphasize the beauty of physical exercise.
- **Unbeatable Record** : Soviet gymnast Larisa Latynina holds 18 Olympic medals, a record she maintained for 48 years until 2012.
- **Youngest Ever** : In 1936, Inge Sørensen of Denmark won a bronze in gymnastics at the tender age of 12, making her one of the youngest medalists in Olympic history.

- **Perfect Ten** : Nadia Comăneci, a Romanian gymnast, scored the first perfect 10 at the Montreal Olympics in 1976. She achieved seven perfect scores in total during these Games.
- **Gravity-defying Vault** : At the 1996 Atlanta Olympics, Kerri Strug performed her final vault with an injured ankle, ensuring gold for the U.S. women's team.
- **Men's Addition** : Although gymnastics was part of the first modern Olympics in 1896, women's gymnastics wasn't introduced until the 1928 Amsterdam Games.
- **Long-standing Champion** : Japanese gymnast Sawao Kato won eight gold medals over three Olympics (1968, 1972, 1976), the most for any male gymnast.
- **Solo Champion** : Czech gymnast Věra Čáslavská is the only gymnast, male or female, to win Olympic gold in every individual event.
- **Age Matters** : Post 1997, female gymnasts must turn 16 during the Olympic year to compete. This rule came into effect after concerns about younger gymnasts' well-being.
- **High-flying Move** : The "Produnova" vault, named after Russian gymnast Elena Produnova, is known as the "vault of death" because of its complexity and the risks involved.
- **Six-time Charm** : Oksana Chusovitina, representing various nations, competed in seven consecutive Olympics from 1992 to 2016, an unmatched record for a gymnast.
- **Diverse Disciplines** : Gymnastics at the Olympics isn't just about artistic events. Rhythmic gymnastics and trampoline were added in 1984 and 2000 respectively.
- **Simone's Dominance** : Simone Biles, with her gravity-defying moves, won four golds at the 2016 Rio Olympics, making her one of the most decorated American gymnasts.
- **Unique Scoring** : The 2008 Beijing Olympics introduced a new scoring system, replacing the iconic 10-point maximum, to make evaluations more transparent and accurate.

- **Identical Score** : At the 2000 Sydney Olympics, Russian and Chinese gymnasts received identical scores. For the first time, both teams shared gold in the women's uneven bars.
- **Legendary Coaching** : Bela and Martha Karolyi coached numerous gymnasts to Olympic glory, spanning several decades and producing champions like Nadia Comăneci and Mary Lou Retton.
- **Return of the Rings** : The rings, initially part of the Olympics, were removed but then reintroduced in 1924, making them one of the few events to have such a history.
- **Continuous Roll** : Romanian women's gymnastics team won gold at every Olympics from 1976 to 2004, a remarkable run of dominance.
- **Resilient Champion** : Hungarian gymnast Ágnes Keleti survived the Holocaust and later went on to win 10 Olympic medals in the 1950s, making her the most successful Jewish Olympian.
- **Rhythmic Exclusivity** : Rhythmic gymnastics is unique as it's the only women-exclusive event in the Olympic Games, with no counterpart for men.

Hammer Throwing

- **Historical Roots** : The origins of hammer throwing can be traced back to the Tailteann Games in Ireland over 2000 years ago. It was only centuries later that it would find its way into modern Olympic competition.
- **Olympic Debut** : Hammer throw made its entrance into the Olympics in the 1900 Paris Games for men. Unfortunately, women would wait over a century for their chance to compete.
- **Women's Entry** : Women were finally allowed to compete in the hammer throw at the Olympics in 2000, Sydney. Before this, they had no official hammer throw event in the Games.

- **Dominant Soviet** : Yuriy Sedykh, a Soviet hammer thrower, won two Olympic golds (1976, 1980) and set an Olympic record of 81.80m in 1980, showcasing his mastery over the event.
- **Safety First** : Originally, the hammer throw involved literally throwing a sledgehammer. The design evolved for better safety, leading to the tethered ball and handle used today.
- **Extended Record** : Anita Włodarczyk, a Polish athlete, won the gold medal in both 2012 and 2016. In Rio 2016, she set an Olympic record with a throw of 82.29m.
- **No Repeat** : Since its Olympic introduction, no country has consecutively won the men's hammer throw more than three times in a row.
- **Hat Trick Champion** : John Flanagan, an Irish-American, clinched three consecutive gold medals in 1900, 1904, and 1908, a feat unmatched to date.
- **Venue Shift** : The hammer throw, due to its danger and required space, is often held outside the main Olympic stadium, a rarity among athletic events.
- **Consistent Technique** : The rotational technique used in modern hammer throwing has remained largely unchanged since the 1950s, showcasing its effectiveness.
- **Double Talent** : Tatyana Lysenko, the Russian hammer thrower who won gold in 2012, also holds the unique distinction of being an accomplished ballet dancer.
- **Notable Absence** : Hammer throw is one of the few track and field events that wasn't part of the first modern Olympics in Athens, 1896.
- **Multiple Medals** : Only three athletes in Olympic history have won three medals in the men's hammer throw, showcasing the event's competitive nature.
- **Impressive Distance** : The cumulative increase in the men's Olympic record, since its inception, is over 30 meters, a testament to the sport's progress.

- **Hefty Implement** : The men's hammer weighs 7.26kg, and the women's is 4kg. Yet, these weights are thrown impressive distances, showcasing sheer power and technique.
- **Shifting Nationalities** : József Csermák, the 1952 gold medalist, was born in Hungary but later represented Spain in international competitions.
- **Unfortunate Ban** : Due to doping scandals, Russian track and field athletes, including hammer throwers, were banned from the 2016 Rio Olympics.
- **Unique Stance** : Hammer throw is the only throwing event in the Olympics where the athlete remains stationary, relying on rotation rather than a run-up.
- **Unmatched Record** : The current men's world record, set by Yuriy Sedykh in 1986 at 86.74m, remains unbroken in Olympic competitions.
- **Dedicated Venue** : Due to its specific needs, the 2012 London Olympics built a temporary venue solely for hammer throw and discus.

High Jump

- **Historical Origins** : The high jump has ancient roots, with evidence suggesting it was practiced in Scotland over 2,000 years ago. This ancestral event made its modern Olympic debut in 1896 for men and 1928 for women.
- **Fosbury Revolution** : The 1968 Mexico City Olympics witnessed Dick Fosbury's unique backward jump technique, now called the "Fosbury Flop." This innovative approach would soon become the dominant style.
- **First Female Gold** : Ethel Catherwood of Canada won the first women's high jump gold in the 1928 Amsterdam Olympics, leaping 1.595m.
- **World Record Holder** : Javier Sotomayor of Cuba, who jumped an astonishing 2.45m in 1993, remains the only man to have

cleared eight feet and still holds the world record, though not set in the Olympics.

- **Olympic Record** : Charles Austin's jump of 2.39m during the 1996 Atlanta Games still stands as the men's Olympic record.
- **Youngest Champion** : Korean athlete Sohn Kee-Chung, at the age of 17, clinched the gold in 1936, making him the youngest male high jump gold medalist.
- **Consecutive Wins** : Iolanda Balaş of Romania stands out, having won consecutive golds in 1960 and 1964 and dominating the women's high jump scene for a decade.
- **Zero Clears** : The 1908 London Olympics witnessed a bizarre event where no female athlete cleared the opening height in the high jump final.
- **Home Advantage** : The 1980 Moscow Games saw 21-year-old Polish jumper Jacek Wszoła set an Olympic record of 2.35m, beating the host nation's favorites.
- **Dual Medalist** : American athlete Mildred "Babe" Didrikson Zaharias showed her prowess in the 1932 Los Angeles Games, clinching gold in the high jump and 80m hurdles.
- **Style Evolution** : Before the Fosbury Flop, athletes jumped using techniques like the scissors jump, Eastern cut-off, and Western roll.
- **Double Gold** : The enigmatic Ethel Catherwood remains the only woman to win Olympic gold in high jump and the British Empire Games in the same year, 1928.
- **Height Progression** : From 1908 to 2016, the Olympic record for the men's high jump improved by a massive 36cm.
- **Hometown Hero** : The 1964 Tokyo Olympics saw Valeriy Brumel, a Soviet athlete, taking gold with a leap of 2.18m, beating American John Thomas by just 2cm.
- **Not Just Height** : The event isn't solely about jumping height. Athletes also have to master the three phases: approach, take-off, and bar clearance.

- **Footwear Evolution** : Athletes in the early 20th century used flat-soled shoes. Modern high jumpers wear specially designed shoes with a thicker sole under the ball of the takeoff foot.
- **Unique Clear** : At the 2000 Sydney Olympics, Stefan Holm of Sweden, standing at 1.81m tall, cleared 2.32m, an exceptional 51cm above his height.
- **Last Jump Triumph** : At the 1960 Rome Olympics, American John Thomas was favored to win but was upset by Robert Shavlakadze of the USSR on his final jump.
- **Photo Finish** : With the advancement of technology, photoelectric cells were introduced in 1972 to determine if an athlete's body had cleared the bar.
- **All-time Best** : Stefka Kostadinova of Bulgaria set the world record in 1987 with 2.09m. This jump, not made during the Olympics, remains unbeaten in women's high jump to date.

Hurdle Race

- **Historical Debut** : Hurdling can trace its Olympic origins back to the second modern Olympic Games in 1900. At that event, only the men's 110m hurdles was contested.
- **Female Introduction** : Women wouldn't contest in Olympic hurdle races until the 1932 Los Angeles Games, with the introduction of the 80m hurdles.
- **First Champion** : Alvin Kraenzlein of the USA won the first Olympic 110m hurdles in 1900, setting a time of 15.4 seconds.
- **Distance Change** : The women's 80m hurdles was extended to 100m for the 1972 Munich Olympics, aligning the race distance with other international competitions.
- **Triple Triumph** : Harrison Dillard of the USA is the only athlete to have won gold in both the 100m sprint (1948) and 110m hurdles (1952).

- **Close Finish** : The 2016 Rio Olympics saw Omar McLeod of Jamaica win the 110m hurdles with just 0.12 seconds separating the gold and bronze medalists.
- **Double Defense** : Sally Pearson of Australia won the women's 100m hurdles at the 2012 London Olympics and successfully defended her title in 2016, demonstrating consistent excellence.
- **Dramatic Fall** : Lolo Jones was a favorite in the 2008 Beijing Olympics but hit the ninth hurdle in the finals, costing her a medal and finishing 7th.
- **Ageless Wonder** : Merlene Ottey competed in the 80m hurdles at the age of 16 in the 1980 Moscow Olympics and continued her Olympic journey until age 40.
- **Staggering Record** : The men's 400m hurdles record of 46.78 seconds set by Kevin Young at the 1992 Barcelona Olympics remains unbeaten in Olympic competition.
- **Dominant Display** : Edwin Moses, a true legend of the 400m hurdles, went unbeaten in 122 races over a decade and won two Olympic golds in 1976 and 1984.
- **Innovative Technique** : Hurdling style has evolved, with athletes like Edwin Moses counting 13 steps between hurdles instead of the traditional 14.
- **Double Feat** : Only Fanny Blankers-Koen (1948) and Shirley Strickland (1952, 1956) have managed to win consecutive Olympic golds in the women's 100m hurdles.
- **Rapid Progress** : From 1900 to 2016, the Olympic record for the men's 110m hurdles improved by an impressive 2.2 seconds.
- **Tightest Margin** : The 2012 London Games saw Aries Merritt win the 110m hurdles by just 0.12 seconds, demonstrating the fine margins of victory.
- **High Hopes Dashed** : World record holder Liu Xiang carried China's hopes in the 2008 Beijing Olympics but had to withdraw from the 110m hurdles due to injury.

- **Adaptable Athlete** : Dalilah Muhammad, primarily a 400m hurdler, also competes in the 4x400m relay, showcasing her versatility.
- **No Triple Gold** : No male athlete has ever won three consecutive gold medals in the 110m hurdles, showcasing the event's competitiveness.
- **Height Matters** : The men's hurdles are set at a height of 42 inches for 110m and 36 inches for 400m, challenging athletes' speed and technique.
- **Barrier Breaker** : Karsten Warholm of Norway smashed the 46-second barrier in the 400m hurdles with a time of 45.94 in 2021, though not set in the Olympics.

Ice Hockey

- **Historical Start** : Ice hockey made its Olympic debut at the 1920 Summer Games in Antwerp, not a Winter Olympics. This was seven years before the first Winter Games in 1924.
- **Female Breakthrough** : Women's ice hockey only joined the Olympic program in 1998 during the Nagano Games, nearly 80 years after the men's debut.
- **Dominant USSR** : From 1956 to 1988, the Soviet Union's men's team clinched gold seven times out of nine Olympic appearances.
- **Miracle on Ice** : In the 1980 Lake Placid Olympics, the underdog US team defeated the heavily favored Soviet squad in a match often termed the "Miracle on Ice".
- **Sudden Growth** : By the time the 2014 Sochi Olympics rolled around, women's ice hockey had expanded to include eight national teams, up from six in its debut.
- **Prolific Scorer** : In the 1924 Olympics, Harry Watson of Canada scored an astounding 36 goals in just five games.
- **Unbeatable Canadians** : The Canadian men's team won six of the first seven Olympic gold medals from 1920 to 1952.

- **Twin Gold** : In the 2014 Sochi Olympics, both the Canadian men's and women's hockey teams clinched gold.
- **Goal Galore** : The most goals ever scored by a team in an Olympic ice hockey game is 33, achieved by Canada against Denmark in 1949.
- **Pioneering Europe** : The first European country to introduce ice hockey was Great Britain, winning its first gold in the 1936 Olympics.
- **Tightest Win** : In the 1994 Lillehammer Olympics, Sweden won the men's ice hockey gold in a dramatic penalty shootout against Canada.
- **Sisters in Skates** : The 2014 Canadian gold-winning team featured three sets of sisters, showcasing familial talent in the sport.
- **Scoreless Defense** : At the 2002 Salt Lake City Olympics, Canada's women's team did not concede a single goal in the group stages.
- **Penalty King** : In 1988, Ray LeBlanc of the USA faced 105 shots and made 102 saves, a 97.14% success rate, one of the highest in Olympic history.
- **Unstoppable Squad** : The 1956 Soviet team scored a remarkable 40 goals and only conceded 7 in 7 games, dominating their Olympic debut.
- **Golden Shutout** : Dominik Hašek, representing the Czech Republic in 1998, recorded two shutouts in the final rounds, leading his team to an unexpected gold.
- **Overtime Drama** : In the 2018 PyeongChang Olympics, the USA women's team defeated Canada in a tense shootout after a 2-2 draw in regulation and overtime.
- **Longest Game** : The longest Olympic ice hockey game lasted 174 minutes and 30 seconds in 1936 when Great Britain defeated France 3-2.

- **Historic Venue** : The 1932 Lake Placid Olympic ice hockey games were held at the Olympic Center, which is now the oldest indoor rink still in use.
- **Comeback Kids** : In 1980, the US team trailed Finland 2-1 after two periods in the gold medal game but roared back to win 4-2, securing their "Miracle on Ice" legacy.

Javelin Throwing

- **Ancient Origins** : The sport of javelin throwing traces back to ancient Greece and was included in the original Olympic Games. It symbolized the hunting and battle prowess of an athlete.
- **Two Techniques** : Before 1956, athletes could choose to throw the javelin either by running up or from a standing position. The running technique became standardized due to its popularity and effectiveness.
- **Shifting Standards** : In 1986, the men's javelin specification was changed because athletes were throwing near the end of the field. The center of gravity was moved 4cm forward to reduce flight distance.
- **Groundbreaking Jan** : Jan Železný of the Czech Republic holds the men's world record with a throw of 98.48m in 1996 and clinched three consecutive Olympic golds (1992, 1996, and 2000).
- **Consistent Osleidys** : Cuba's Osleidys Menéndez set a women's world record in 2001 with 71.70m, and subsequently won Olympic gold in Athens 2004 with an Olympic record throw of 71.53m.
- **Versatile Athlete** : Bud Held from the USA, who introduced the first hollow javelin, was not only a top thrower but also innovated equipment designs in the 1950s.
- **Longest Reign** : Uwe Hohn's 104.80m throw in 1984 stands unbeaten due to the subsequent change in javelin specifications. He remains the only man to throw over 100m.

- **Notable Rivalry** : In the 2008 Beijing Olympics, Tero Pitkämäki and Andreas Thorkildsen's duel was legendary, with the Norwegian Thorkildsen taking the gold.
- **A Perfect Finish** : In 2012, Keshorn Walcott of Trinidad and Tobago won gold in his Olympic debut, becoming the first from the Western Hemisphere outside the US to win the men's javelin throw.
- **Close Call** : In 1932, both the gold and silver medalists, Matti Järvinen and Matti Sippala, represented Finland, differing by a mere 45 centimeters in their throws.
- **Double Talents** : Ellina Zvereva from Belarus won gold in discus at 2000 Sydney Olympics but earlier in her career, she competed in the javelin throw during the 1988 Seoul Olympics.
- **Transformation** : Women's javelin underwent a design change in 1999, moving the center of gravity 4cm forward, mirroring the men's change years prior.
- **German Dominance** : In the 2016 Rio Olympics, Germany took all three medals in the women's javelin, showcasing their national strength in the discipline.
- **Two in a Row** : In 1988 and 1992, Petra Felke of East Germany and then Germany won consecutive Olympic golds in the women's javelin.
- **Making History** : Cy Young, apart from being a baseball legend, won the javelin gold in the 1952 Olympics, being the only person with the same name as the baseball award.
- **Iron Curtain Talent** : From 1956 to 1980, athletes from Eastern Bloc countries won every gold medal in the men's javelin throw.
- **The Javelin Dance** : After every successful throw, Kenya's Julius Yego would break into a celebratory dance, earning him considerable fan affection during the 2016 Rio Olympics.
- **Safety First** : Post the 1980 Moscow Olympics, officials began using a sector field instead of a center line for judging throws, decreasing the risk of errant javelins hitting the ground near officials.

- **Young Prodigy** : Tero Pitkämäki won bronze in the 2008 Beijing Olympics, but a year prior, at just 24, he had already thrown a massive 91.53m in the World Championships.
- **Distance Evolution** : The first Olympic record recognized in the men's javelin was 60.64m in 1908. A century later, the Olympic record had evolved to 90.57m, showcasing the development of technique and athleticism.

Judo

- **Introduction** : Judo was introduced to the Olympic Games in 1964 in Tokyo, Japan. This inclusion was fitting as judo originated in Japan and the Games served as a global platform for its showcase.
- **Pioneering Women** : Women first took part in Olympic judo during a demonstration event in 1988 in Seoul. They officially joined in the Barcelona 1992 Olympics, expanding the sport's reach and diversity.
- **Clean Sweep** : Japan, the birthplace of judo, dominated the inaugural 1964 Olympic event by winning three of the four available gold medals.
- **Non-Stop Teddy** : Teddy Riner from France has won 2 Olympic gold medals and has remained unbeaten in international competitions from 2010 to 2020, solidifying his legendary status.
- **Double Delight** : Only five judokas have won three Olympic gold medals: Tadahiro Nomura (Japan), Hitoshi Saito (Japan), Ryoko Tani (Japan), Ilias Iliadis (Greece), and Teddy Riner (France).
- **Sibling Success** : The Kosei brothers, Inoue and Uchishiba, have both won Olympic gold medals for Japan, showcasing their family's prowess in the sport.
- **Youthful Triumph** : Ilias Iliadis won his first Olympic gold at the tender age of 17 in the 2004 Athens Olympics, making him one of the youngest judo champions.

- **Diverse Dominance** : Since its inclusion, judo gold medals have been won by athletes from over 30 different countries, illustrating the sport's global appeal and competitive nature.
- **Paralympic Parallel** : Judo is one of the few martial arts included in the Paralympics. Since 1988, visually impaired judokas have showcased their skills on this global stage.
- **Lightning Fast** : At the 2000 Sydney Olympics, Ryoko Tani won one of her matches in a mere 12 seconds, displaying her unparalleled skill and reflexes.
- **Historic Exclusion** : Curiously, after its 1964 debut, judo was excluded from the 1968 Mexico City Olympics. It made its return in 1972 and has been a staple since.
- **Extra Chances** : Unlike many Olympic sports, in judo, athletes who lose to a finalist get a chance to compete again for a bronze medal via the repechage system.
- **Instant Impact** : Kosovo made its Olympic debut in 2016 and achieved immediate success with Majlinda Kelmendi winning gold in the women's 52kg judo event.
- **Size Matters** : Judo is one of the few sports where athletes are categorized by their weight rather than age, ensuring evenly matched contests.
- **Historic Venue** : In the 2020 Tokyo Olympics, judo events took place in the Nippon Budokan, the same historic venue where judo debuted in the 1964 Olympics.
- **Unified Korea** : At the 2018 World Judo Championships, North and South Korea's teams competed under a unified flag, promoting peace and unity through sport.
- **Mighty Mongolia** : Mongolia, a nation with a rich history in combat sports, won its first Olympic gold in 2008 in judo, thanks to Naidangiin Tüvshinbayar.
- **Noble Gesture** : In the 2016 Olympics, Egyptian judoka Islam El Shehaby was under the spotlight for refusing to shake hands with his Israeli opponent. The act became a topic of debate about sportsmanship and politics.

- **Late Bloomer** : France's Lucie Décosse won her first Olympic gold at age 30 in the London 2012 Olympics, proving age is just a number in the pursuit of excellence.
- **Fair Play** : Judo places a significant emphasis on respect and etiquette. The Olympic matches start and end with a bow, underscoring the sport's values of honor and humility.

Long Jump

- **Ancient Roots** : The long jump was a key component of the ancient Olympic Games in Greece starting in 708 BC. Athletes used weights called "halteres" to assist their jump.
- **Remarkable Bob** : Bob Beamon's 1968 Mexico City leap was so long, it exceeded the official measuring equipment's capability. His jump of 8.90 meters remained a record for 23 years.
- **Versatile Lewis** : Carl Lewis won the long jump gold medal in four consecutive Olympics from 1984 to 1996, showcasing unparalleled dominance in the event.
- **Historic Jump** : The first modern Olympic Games in 1896 had the long jump event, making it one of the original modern Olympic sports.
- **Women's Entry** : Women began competing in the Olympic long jump in 1948 in London. This addition helped push gender equality in Olympic sports forward.
- **Barefoot Champion** : Ethel Catherwood, often known as the "Saskatoon Lily", won the 1928 women's long jump event jumping barefoot, which was unusual even for her time.
- **High Altitude** : The 1968 Mexico City Olympics were held at high altitude, which many believe helped athletes achieve longer jumps due to thin air resistance.
- **Consistent Jackie** : Jackie Joyner-Kersee, known for her heptathlon exploits, also secured two gold medals and a silver in the long jump between 1988 and 1996.

- **Narrow Margins** : At the 1984 Los Angeles Olympics, Carl Lewis won by the smallest margin in Olympic history: just 1 cm separated him from the silver medalist.
- **Closest Battle** : In 2004, the top three women in the long jump were separated by only 3 centimeters, showcasing the intense competition of the sport.
- **Runway Length** : The Olympic long jump runway is typically 40 meters long, giving athletes ample distance to gain speed and momentum for their leap.
- **Double Gold** : In 1936, Jesse Owens won both the 100m and the long jump, making a significant political and athletic statement during the Berlin Games.
- **Stunning Debut** : Lynn Davies from Britain, nicknamed "Lynn the Leap", won gold on his Olympic debut in 1964 in Tokyo.
- **Wind Assistance** : For a record to be considered legal in long jump at the Olympics, the tailwind cannot exceed 2.0 meters per second.
- **Footwear Evolution** : In the early 20th century, jumpers landed feet first, leading to specialized shoes being developed by 1928 to aid in this technique.
- **Pit Specs** : The sandpit for the Olympic long jump must be at least 2.75 meters wide and 10 meters long, ensuring jumpers' safety and accuracy.
- **Multiple Medals** : Heike Drechsler of Germany secured long jump medals in three separate Olympics: gold in 1992 and 2000, and silver in 1988.
- **Leap and Sprint** : Many athletes have successfully combined sprinting and long jumping in the Olympics, including legends like Carl Lewis and Jesse Owens.
- **Consistency** : The U.S. holds the most long jump gold medals in Olympic history for both men and women, demonstrating consistent prowess in the event.

- **Shortest Record** : The shortest world record jump accepted under modern judging conditions was 7.61 meters by Peter O'Connor in 1901, showcasing how the sport has progressed.

Marathon

- **Historic Origins** : The marathon commemorates the run of the soldier Pheidippides from a battlefield near Marathon, Greece, to Athens in 490 B.C. This historic run signaled the Greeks' victory over the Persians.
- **First Event** : The marathon made its Olympic debut during the first modern Games in 1896. Spiridon Louis of Greece emerged as the inaugural winner.
- **Distance Standardization** : The marathon's official distance, 42.195 kilometers (26.219 miles), was standardized at the 1908 London Olympics. The distance was set to accommodate the British royal family's viewing of the start and finish.
- **Women's Strides** : Women's marathon was included much later in the Olympics, with its debut in the 1984 Los Angeles Games. Joan Benoit of the USA claimed the first gold.
- **Golden Abebe** : Abebe Bikila of Ethiopia became the first Black African Olympic champion by winning the marathon in Rome 1960, and he did it running barefoot!
- **Back-to-Back Wins** : Only a handful of marathoners, including Waldemar Cierpinski and Abebe Bikila, have won back-to-back Olympic marathon gold medals.
- **Scorching Conditions** : The 1900 Paris Olympics marathon was contested under brutal 39°C heat. Most of the competitors didn't finish, emphasizing the marathon's extreme challenges.
- **Fueling Finish** : During the 1904 St. Louis Olympics, Thomas Hicks was given a mixture of strychnine and brandy to help him finish the race. He won, but had to be carried off the track.

- **Ageless Champion** : At 37, Carlos Lopes of Portugal became the oldest Olympic marathon winner in 1984. His victory remains an inspiration for many.
- **Spectacular Scenery** : The 2004 Athens Olympic marathon retraced the ancient course from Marathon to Athens, offering participants a scenic and historic route.
- **Mizuki's Grit** : Mizuki Noguchi of Japan secured the gold in the women's marathon at Athens 2004, becoming the first Asian woman to win the event.
- **Dramatic Finish** : At the 1908 London Olympics, Dorando Pietri of Italy entered the stadium disoriented, collapsing multiple times but was helped over the line, leading to his eventual disqualification.
- **Youngest Runner** : Dimitrios Loundras was only 10 years old when he participated in the team parallel bars event at the inaugural 1896 Games, making him the youngest known Olympic marathoner.
- **World Records** : The Olympic Games has not been a frequent venue for world records in the marathon, given the varying courses and conditions.
- **Unusual Marathon** : The 1904 Olympic marathon saw multiple peculiar incidents including feral dogs chasing runners and competitors hitching rides.
- **Kipchoge's Legend** : Eliud Kipchoge of Kenya, known for breaking the 2-hour marathon barrier in a special event, also secured gold in both the 2016 and 2020 Olympic marathons.
- **Surprising Silver** : In 2000, Eritrea's Zersenay Tadese, primarily known as a track runner, stunned many by securing a marathon silver at the Beijing Olympics.
- **Late Bloomer** : Constantina Diță of Romania was 38 when she clinched gold at the 2008 Beijing Olympic marathon, proving age is but a number.

- **Marathon Mass** : 1972 marked the largest number of competitors in an Olympic marathon with 74 nations participating, highlighting the event's global appeal.
- **Heroic Fails** : In 1912, Japan's Shizo Kanakuri abandoned his marathon due to heat and went home without informing officials. He completed his race in 1967, making his marathon time 54 years, 8 months, 6 days, 5 hours, 32 minutes, and 20.379 seconds!

Modern Pentathlon

- **Inception** : The modern pentathlon was introduced by the founder of the modern Olympics, Pierre de Coubertin, in 1912. He believed it would test a person's moral qualities and physical abilities.
- **Five Disciplines** : This event combines five disciplines: fencing, freestyle swimming, equestrian show jumping, pistol shooting, and cross-country running. It's designed to mimic the experience of a 19th-century cavalry soldier behind enemy lines.
- **Swedish Dominance** : Sweden has won the most Olympic gold medals in this discipline, with a total of 9 golds as of 2021.
- **All-in-One** : Since 2009, the running and shooting events were combined, echoing the biathlon in the Winter Olympics.
- **Historic Origins** : The concept of the pentathlon is ancient, dating back to the original Olympic Games in Greece, where it comprised discus, javelin, long jump, wrestling, and a foot race.
- **First Woman** : The women's event in the modern pentathlon was only introduced relatively recently, at the 2000 Sydney Olympics.
- **Shortest Duration** : Of all the multi-discipline Olympic events, the modern pentathlon has the shortest competition duration, typically lasting just one day.
- **Decisive Moment** : At the 1976 Montreal Games, Boris Onishchenko of the Soviet Union was disqualified for rigging his

épée to register hits when there weren't any, causing a major scandal.

- **World Leader** : As of 2021, Hungary leads the all-time medal count in the Olympic modern pentathlon with 22 medals, showcasing their consistent excellence.
- **Olympic Exclusivity** : Unlike many other Olympic sports, the modern pentathlon is almost exclusively an Olympic event, with few major competitions outside of the Games.
- **High Demands** : Athletes spend approximately 4-5 hours competing across the five disciplines, demanding unparalleled endurance and versatility.
- **Fencing Marathon** : In the fencing round-robin, athletes might face up to 35 bouts, each one minute in duration.
- **Equestrian Challenge** : Athletes don't ride their own horses. Instead, they're paired with an unfamiliar horse just 20 minutes before competing, testing adaptability.
- **Shooting Pressure** : In the combined shooting and running event, athletes must hit five targets in 50 seconds before setting off on each running leg.
- **Youthful Champion** : In 2012, David Svoboda of the Czech Republic set an Olympic record with 5,928 points, showcasing the sport's evolution.
- **Sport's Sage** : At 52, Hungary's András Balczó was the oldest gold medal winner in the modern pentathlon at the Munich 1972 Olympics.
- **Noteworthy Venue** : The 2012 London Olympics held the pentathlon events in the Greenwich Park, an UNESCO World Heritage site, blending history with modern competition.
- **Changing Formats** : The format of the modern pentathlon has changed six times since its introduction in 1912, reflecting its evolving nature.
- **Golden Debut** : Stephanie Cook of Great Britain won the gold medal during the women's modern pentathlon debut at the 2000 Sydney Olympics.

- **Rare Repeat** : No athlete has ever won consecutive gold medals in the Olympic modern pentathlon, highlighting the event's unpredictability and competition.

Nordic Combined

- **Origins** : Nordic combined, a combination of cross-country skiing and ski jumping, has its roots in Norway. Historically, it's been considered the ultimate test of Nordic skiing skills.
- **Debut** : Making its Olympic debut at the first Winter Games in Chamonix 1924, the Nordic combined has been an essential part of every Winter Olympics since.
- **Sole Domain** : For 84 years, only men participated in the event. Women finally got their event in the 2022 Beijing Winter Olympics.
- **Legendary Streak** : Norway has consistently excelled in Nordic combined, boasting a total of 30 Olympic medals by 2021.
- **Two-in-One** : Originally, there was just one individual Nordic combined event. But by the 1988 Calgary Winter Olympics, the team event was added.
- **Ski Change** : In the initial editions of the Games, participants used the same pair of skis for both jumping and cross-country. Now, athletes have specialized skis for each discipline.
- **Gundersen** : The "Gundersen Method," adopted in 1988, involves a points-based calculation to determine the start of the cross-country race based on the ski jumping results.
- **Iconic Venue** : The Holmenkollen ski arena in Oslo, Norway, one of the most iconic venues in the sport, has never hosted an Olympic event but has been pivotal in shaping champions.
- **French Exception** : Jason Lamy-Chappuis, born in Montana, USA but representing France, won the gold in 2010 Vancouver Games, highlighting the sport's global appeal.
- **Fierce Competition** : No athlete has ever won more than two gold medals in Olympic Nordic combined competitions, demonstrating the fierce level of competition.

- **Distances Evolve** : The cross-country skiing distance was initially 18 km. It changed several times and is now 10 km for individuals and 4 x 5 km for teams.
- **Soaring Record** : Austria set a remarkable record at the 2010 Vancouver Games by winning all three Nordic combined gold medals.
- **Unfamiliar Terrain** : The 1998 Nagano Games saw the first time Nordic combined was held on Asian soil.
- **Turbulent Weather** : During the 1960 Squaw Valley Games, fierce winds disrupted the ski jumping segment, causing it to be postponed.
- **Triumphant Return** : After a 16-year hiatus from the top podium, Finland clinched gold in the team event at the 2018 PyeongChang Games.
- **All-Rounder** : Johan Grøttumsbraaten of Norway is the only athlete to have won both individual and team events in Nordic combined at the same Olympic Games, achieving this feat in 1928.
- **Decisive Seconds** : At the 2014 Sochi Games, Norway's Joergen Graabak beat Germany's Fabian Riessle by just 0.6 seconds in one of the tightest finishes ever.
- **Venue Shifts** : The 1932 Lake Placid Games saw the cross-country segment being moved to a different location due to lack of snow.
- **Dominant Era** : From 1924 to 1936, only two nations, Norway and Finland, won all the Nordic combined medals available.
- **Triple Threat** : Ulrich Wehling of East Germany is the only athlete to have won three consecutive golds in individual Nordic combined (1972, 1976, and 1980).

Pole Vault

- **Origins** : The pole vault's roots trace back to ancient times where Greeks used poles to leap over bulls. The sport evolved into what we recognize today by the 19th century.
- **Olympic Debut** : Men's pole vaulting was introduced to the Olympics during the inaugural 1896 Athens Games. It would take another 100 years for women to get their event in 2000.
- **Height Evolution** : In the 1896 Olympics, the winning height was 3.30m. By contrast, the world record by 2021 stood at an astounding 6.18m by Armand Duplantis.
- **Barrier Break** : Sergei Bubka of the Soviet Union was the first man to clear the 6-meter mark in 1985, reshaping the ambitions of vaulters everywhere.
- **Dominance** : The USA has historically dominated the men's pole vault, with over 20 Olympic medals to their name by 2021.
- **Perfect Tens** : By the 2004 Athens Games, Yelena Isinbayeva became the first woman to clear the 5-meter mark, setting a new standard for female vaulters.
- **Ceiling Smash** : In the 2016 Rio Olympics, Thiago Braz da Silva broke the Olympic record by clearing 6.03 meters.
- **Wartime Hiatus** : The pole vault, like many Olympic events, faced interruptions due to World Wars. The 1916, 1940, and 1944 Games were all canceled.
- **Material Evolution** : Vaulters initially used bamboo poles. The shift to fiberglass in the 1960s revolutionized the sport, allowing for greater heights.
- **Indoor Feat** : In 2014, Renaud Lavillenie of France set an indoor world record of 6.16 meters, surpassing Bubka's long-standing mark.
- **Consistency King** : Bob Richards is the only man to have won back-to-back Olympic golds in pole vaulting (1952 and 1956).
- **Defying Age** : At 41, Svetlana Feofanova competed in the 2016 Rio Olympics, showcasing the longevity possible in the sport.

- **Unique Hat-trick** : Yelena Isinbayeva is the only woman to win the Olympic pole vault title twice and set 17 world records in her career.
- **Surprising Silver** : The 1960 Rome Olympics saw a non-American, Don Bragg, win gold, while the favorite, Ron Morris, took silver.
- **Sandpit Switch** : Initially, vaulters landed in sandpits. Safety mats were introduced in the 1960s, greatly reducing injury risks.
- **Remarkable Comeback** : After finishing 21st in 2012, Brazil's da Silva clinched gold in 2016, demonstrating the unpredictability and drama inherent in the event.
- **Gender Milestone** : The 2000 Sydney Games marked the first time women participated in Olympic pole vaulting, with Stacy Dragila taking gold.
- **Aerial Ballet** : The "rock-back" technique, where the vaulter arches their back and swings upward, was popularized in the 1960s, adding an aesthetic appeal to the athletic feat.
- **Vaulting Versatility** : Athlete E. E. Barnard won the 1900 Paris Olympics pole vault, and in a display of versatility, also clinched silver in the standing high jump.
- **Record Reign** : Sergei Bubka's outdoor world record of 6.14 meters, set in 1994, stood unbroken for over two decades until 2020.

Road Racing

- **Inception** : Road racing made its Olympic debut at the inaugural modern Olympic Games in Athens in 1896. This marked the beginning of a storied relationship between the Games and road cycling disciplines.
- **Marathon Ride** : The 1984 Los Angeles Olympics featured an astonishing 190.2 km men's road race. Alexi Grewal of the USA won in a thrilling sprint finish.

- **Pioneering Women** : Women's road racing wasn't included in the Olympic program until the 1984 Los Angeles Games. Connie Carpenter-Phinney claimed the first gold medal for the event.
- **Back-to-Back** : Paolo Bettini of Italy won consecutive gold medals in the men's road race in 2004 and 2008, showcasing his dominance in the discipline.
- **High Altitude** : The 1968 Mexico City Olympics road race was challenging due to its altitude at over 2,300 meters above sea level, presenting unique difficulties for the cyclists.
- **Diverse Terrain** : The Rio 2016 road race included everything from flat beachside stretches to mountainous terrains, testing cyclists' adaptability.
- **Time Trials** : The individual time trial, where cyclists race against the clock, was added to the Olympics in 1996 in Atlanta. This allowed riders to showcase their pacing and endurance.
- **Record Pace** : At the 2012 London Olympics, Bradley Wiggins completed the men's time trial at a blistering average speed of 52.52 km/h, earning gold.
- **Rare Feat** : Only two athletes, Jeannie Longo of France and Leontien van Moorsel of the Netherlands, have won the women's road race twice in Olympic history.
- **Narrow Margins** : At the 2016 Rio Olympics, Anna van der Breggen won the women's road race by a mere 1.14 seconds, exemplifying the race's fierce competitiveness.
- **Youngest Victor** : At 19 years old, Marianne Vos of the Netherlands clinched silver in the women's road race during the 2004 Athens Olympics.
- **Country Dominance** : Italy boasts a record of five gold medals in men's road racing from the inception of the Olympics through 2021.
- **Twin Victory** : In the 2016 Rio Olympics, brothers Simon and Adam Yates both represented Great Britain in the road race, marking a rare sibling pairing in the event.

- **World and Olympic Champ** : Anna van der Breggen achieved a rare double by becoming both the World Champion and Olympic gold medalist in 2020.
- **Close Calls** : Fabian Cancellara, in the 2016 Rio Olympics men's time trial, beat runner-up Tom Dumoulin by a mere 47.41 seconds over a 54.56 km course.
- **Survival Test** : The 1928 Amsterdam Olympics road race was a staggering 168 km, testing the stamina and endurance of every competitor.
- **Historic Venue** : The 2012 London Olympics road race started and finished at the iconic The Mall, with Buckingham Palace as a backdrop.
- **Tireless Effort** : Clara Hughes, a Canadian cyclist, is the only athlete to have won multiple medals in both the Winter (in speed skating) and Summer Olympics (in road cycling).
- **Racing Return** : Road racing, after being absent in the 1912 Stockholm Olympics, made a triumphant return in the 1920 Antwerp Games.
- **Golden Debut** : Nicole Cooke of Great Britain, in her first Olympics appearance in 2008, clinched gold in the women's road race, marking a stellar Olympic debut.

Rowing

- **Debut** : Rowing was introduced to the Olympic program in 1900, at the Paris Games. Since then, it has been an integral part of the Summer Olympics.
- **Women's Entry** : The 1976 Montreal Olympics saw the inclusion of women's rowing events. Previously, only men competed in this strenuous discipline.
- **Staggering Distances** : Olympic rowing races cover 2,000 meters. Athletes have to balance speed with stamina over this demanding distance.

- **Record Timing** : In 2012, at the London Olympics, the New Zealand pair of Hamish Bond and Eric Murray finished in just 6:08.50, setting a new Olympic record.
- **Photo Finish** : The 1924 Paris Olympics had a nail-biting finish in the men's eights, with Italy edging out Switzerland by a mere 0.2 seconds.
- **Dominant Force** : The British duo of Steve Redgrave and Matthew Pinsent collectively won 9 Olympic gold medals from 1984 to 2004, showcasing unparalleled dominance in the sport.
- **Lightweight Category** : The 1996 Atlanta Olympics introduced lightweight rowing events. These events ensured that those under a certain weight could compete on an even playing field.
- **Diverse Venues** : Olympic rowing has taken place on diverse water bodies, from artificial lakes like Eton Dorney in 2012 to natural courses like Lake Wendouree in 1956.
- **Eightfold Challenge** : The "eights" is the largest rowing event, with 9 athletes – 8 rowers and a coxswain. This event requires immense coordination and teamwork.
- **Weather Challenges** : The 1912 Stockholm Olympics witnessed rowing events being postponed due to strong winds, highlighting the sport's vulnerability to nature's whims.
- **Age No Bar** : At the age of 40, Steve Redgrave won his fifth consecutive gold medal in rowing at the 2000 Sydney Olympics, proving age is just a number.
- **Country Dominance** : The United States dominated men's eights, winning gold consecutively from 1920 to 1956.
- **Marathon Row** : The 1900 Paris Olympics had an unusual rowing distance of about 1,750 meters, compared to the standard 2,000 meters today.
- **Closest Margin** : In the 2004 Athens Olympics, the women's quadruple sculls saw Germany beat Great Britain by just 0.08 seconds.

- **Missing Coxswain** : In the 1904 St. Louis Olympics, the winning team in coxed pairs had a coxswain who was replaced by a teenager they found on the spot!
- **Continental First** : El Salvador won its first Olympic medal in rowing, when Salvadoran rower Carlos Palacios captured bronze in the men's single sculls at the 2002 Athens Olympics.
- **Double Gold** : Romano Battisti and Francesco Fossi of Italy secured gold in both the men's lightweight double sculls and the men's lightweight coxless four at the 2016 Rio de Janeiro Olympics.
- **Sweeping & Sculling** : Rowing at the Olympics comprises two main techniques: sweeping (one oar per rower) and sculling (two oars per rower), challenging athletes in varied disciplines.
- **Quadruple Challenge** : The quadruple sculls event, which requires four athletes each using two oars, made its Olympic debut for men in 1976 and for women in 1988.
- **Ever-present** : Rowing has been present in every edition of the Summer Olympics since its introduction, except for 1896 due to bad weather conditions.

Rugby Sevens

- **Recent Inclusion** : Rugby sevens made its Olympic debut in 2016 at the Rio de Janeiro Games. This added a fast-paced variant of the sport to the Olympic roster.
- **Historical Predecessor** : Traditional 15-a-side rugby was previously played in the Olympics but was last featured in 1924. The inclusion of sevens brought rugby back after a 92-year hiatus.
- **Dominant Fiji** : The Fijian men's team won their country's first-ever Olympic medal at the 2016 Games in Rio. Notably, it was a gold.
- **New Zealand's Pride** : The New Zealand women's team clinched gold at the Tokyo 2020 Olympics, showcasing their dominance in the sport.

- **Quick Pace** : Rugby sevens matches in the Olympics are notably short, lasting just 14 minutes (two halves of 7 minutes each), making every second count.
- **Stadium Filled** : Deodoro Stadium in Rio saw an attendance of over 60,000 fans for the rugby sevens finals in 2016, highlighting the sport's popularity.
- **Unified Team** : The 2016 Rio Olympics saw Great Britain fielding a unified team, with players from England, Scotland, and Wales.
- **Double Victory** : In the 2020 Tokyo Olympics, Fiji's men's team repeated their gold-winning performance from 2016, marking consecutive victories.
- **Sudden Death** : Overtime in rugby sevens at the Olympics employs a "sudden death" rule. The first team to score in overtime wins.
- **Sibling Pride** : In 2016, the Australian women's team featured two sets of sisters, making it a unique family affair on the Olympic stage.
- **Versatile Venue** : The Tokyo 2020 rugby sevens matches were played in the Tokyo Stadium, which also hosted football matches and modern pentathlon events.
- **Historic Win** : The USA men's rugby sevens team achieved their highest-ever Olympic finish at Tokyo 2020, placing sixth.
- **Cap Limit** : In the Olympic format, each team can have a squad of 12 players, with only 7 on the field at once, demanding strategic rotations.
- **Double Try** : At the 2016 Rio Olympics, Dan Norton of Great Britain scored two tries in a match against Kenya, showcasing individual brilliance.
- **Winning Margin** : Australia's women's team defeated New Zealand with a margin of 24-17 in the 2016 final, a significant gap in such a short game format.
- **Pre-Olympic Preparation** : Ahead of the 2016 Olympics, many rugby sevens teams, including the USA, held special training camps to acclimate to Brazil's weather conditions.

- **Prominent Ambassador** : Rugby legend Jonah Lomu, before his untimely passing, was a global ambassador for rugby sevens' inclusion in the Olympics.
- **Injury Management** : Given the sport's intense nature, each team at the Tokyo 2020 Olympics was allowed two traveling reserves to manage potential injuries.
- **Tireless Defense** : At the Tokyo 2020 Olympics, the Argentine men's team had an incredible defensive record, conceding zero tries in their group stage match against South Korea.
- **Global Growth** : Rugby sevens' inclusion in the Olympics has led to increased global participation, with nations like Kenya and Spain showcasing competitive teams on the grand stage.

Short Track Speed Skating

- **Introduction** : Short track speed skating was introduced as a demonstration sport at the 1988 Calgary Winter Olympics. Four years later, in Albertville, it achieved full medal status.
- **Origin** : Although speed skating has early origins in the Netherlands from the 13th century, the short track variant emerged in North America in the 20th century as a way to bring the sport indoors.
- **Close Calls** : The sport's tight track of only 111.12 meters makes for incredibly close and thrilling races, often decided by mere milliseconds.
- **Unpredictability** : At the 2002 Salt Lake City Games, Australian Steven Bradbury won gold in the 1000m after all of his competitors crashed on the last turn, showcasing the sport's unpredictability.
- **Dominance** : South Korea has been particularly dominant in this sport, winning over 45 Olympic medals since its inception as an official Olympic sport.

- **Synchronized Chaos** : A maximum of six skaters participate in each race, navigating tight corners and overtaking challenges on such a small track.
- **Protective Gear** : Due to the sport's high collision risk, athletes wear a range of protective gear, including cut-resistant suits, safety helmets, and knee pads.
- **Photo Finishes** : The 500m men's final at the 2014 Sochi Olympics saw three of the four medalists separated by just .074 seconds, highlighting the importance of photo finishes.
- **Gender Balance** : The 1988 Calgary demonstration events were only for men. However, by the Albertville 1992 Games, both men and women competed for medals.
- **Track Maintenance** : The ice temperature is meticulously kept at -7°C to ensure optimal skating conditions.
- **High Altitude** : At the 1992 Albertville Games, short track events were held at a high-altitude location, potentially giving altitude-trained athletes an advantage.
- **Team Strategy** : The relay event, with teams of four skaters, demands not only speed but also tactical changes and teamwork.
- **Continual Growth** : Since its official Olympic debut in 1992, the number of short track events has expanded from four to eight.
- **Notable Streak** : Viktor Ahn, originally from South Korea but later representing Russia, holds 6 gold medals spanning 3 Olympic Games (2006, 2014, and 2018).
- **Frequent Falls** : Due to the tight corners and aggressive overtaking, falls are common. This led to the creation of the rule that skaters causing intentional interference are disqualified.
- **Instant Replay** : Technology plays a pivotal role in the sport, with referees using instant replay to ensure fair play during close contests.
- **Rapid Start** : The starting shot is crucial. At the 2018 PyeongChang Games, a false start in the men's 500m final led to a skater's disqualification.

- **Young Talent** : At the age of 15, China's Yang Yang participated in her first Olympics in 1998, eventually becoming one of the sport's most decorated athletes.
- **Olympic Record** : The 500m men's Olympic record, set at the 2018 PyeongChang Games by Wu Dajing of China, stands at an astonishing 39.584 seconds.
- **Tight Formation** : Due to the short track's nature, skaters often employ a drafting strategy, staying close behind opponents to minimize air resistance and save energy for final sprints.

Shot Put

- **Introduction** : The shot put, a staple track and field event, has been part of the modern Olympic Games since its inception in 1896 for men, and since 1948 for women.
- **Ancient Origins** : The concept of throwing heavy objects for distance has roots in the Scottish Highlands and ancient civilizations, but the modern circular form was standardized in the 19th century.
- **Record Distance** : In the 1996 Atlanta Olympics, Randy Barnes of the USA set a still-standing Olympic record for men with a throw of 21.62 meters.
- **Techniques** : While the basic concept is simple, athletes use different techniques like the "glide" and the "spin" to optimize their throws.
- **Weight** : Men's shot weighs a substantial 7.26 kilograms, while the women's shot is 4 kilograms.
- **Consistency** : Soviet athlete Tamara Press won the women's shot put in both the 1960 and 1964 Olympics, showcasing her dominance.
- **Nelson's Streak** : American Adam Nelson competed in three Olympics (2000, 2004, and 2008) before finally winning gold in 2004 by a mere 3 centimeters.

- **Two-Event Dominance** : Some athletes, like American Parry O'Brien, have excelled in both the shot put and discus events, demonstrating their versatile strength.
- **Venue** : Shot put events were historically held in ancient-style arenas, but at the 2012 London Olympics, it took place in the spectacular surroundings of The Mall.
- **Spin Evolution** : The rotational or "spin" technique was popularized in the 1970s and revolutionized the sport, allowing for greater distances.
- **Rare Achievement** : Only two men have won back-to-back Olympic shot put titles, and one of them is the legendary Parry O'Brien.
- **Outdoor Challenge** : Unlike other events, shot putters have to contend with outdoor conditions, as the event is never held indoors at the Olympics.
- **Fair Play** : In 2016, New Zealand's Valerie Adams was retroactively awarded gold from the 2012 London Games after the initial winner was disqualified for doping.
- **Continuous Presence** : The men's shot put event has been continuously present at every modern Summer Olympics.
- **Closest Margin** : The 1984 Los Angeles Olympics witnessed the closest margin in Olympic history, with Italian Alessandro Andrei winning by just 1 centimeter.
- **Young Prodigy** : Randy Barnes was only 22 when he won silver at the Seoul Olympics in 1988, showcasing the young talent in this field.
- **Notable Rivalry** : The 2016 Rio Olympics saw Americans Ryan Crouser and Joe Kovacs battling fiercely, with Crouser emerging with gold and an Olympic record of 22.52 meters.
- **Legendary Streak** : Soviet athlete Natalya Lisovskaya won every major shot put event between 1985 and 1988, including the Olympics.

- **Athlete Longevity** : Due to the nature of the event, many shot putters, like John Godina of the USA, have long careers, competing in multiple Olympic Games.
- **Disqualification Turnaround** : In the 2004 Athens Olympics, an initial disqualification for a foot fault in the qualifying rounds was overturned, allowing American Adam Nelson to compete and eventually win silver.

Shot Put

- **Antiquity** : The concept of throwing stones as a test of strength can be traced back to ancient Celtic and Germanic cultures. The formalized sport we know today, however, has its origins in Middle Ages Scotland.
- **Debut** : Men have been competing in the Olympic shot put since the first modern games in Athens, 1896. It was only in the London Olympics of 1948 that women got their chance.
- **Massive Shots** : Men's Olympic shot putters heave a hefty 7.26-kilogram metal ball, whereas women compete with a 4-kilogram version.
- **Record Throw** : At the 2016 Rio de Janeiro Olympics, American Ryan Crouser broke the Olympic record with a phenomenal throw of 22.52 meters.
- **Technique Revolution** : Until the 1950s, most athletes used the 'standing put'. Today, techniques like the 'glide' and 'spin' are more popular and effective.
- **Spin's Birth** : The 'spin' technique was innovated by American athlete Brian Oldfield in 1972. This technique radically transformed the sport's dynamics.
- **Two in a Row** : Only two men, Ralph Rose and Parry O'Brien, have ever won consecutive Olympic gold medals in shot put, showcasing the event's competitiveness.

- **Rivalry** : During the Cold War, an intense rivalry developed between U.S. and USSR shot putters. This competition spurred many record-breaking throws.
- **Consistency** : Soviet athlete Natalya Lisovskaya never lost a major shot put event between 1985 and 1988, proving her unparalleled dominance.
- **Fair Play** : The shot put community emphasizes clean competition. When the 2012 women's gold medalist was found guilty of doping, New Zealand's Valerie Adams was rightly awarded her medal.
- **Age No Barrier** : In 2016, two-time Olympic champion Valerie Adams competed just months after giving birth, highlighting the resilience of shot put athletes.
- **Historical Venues** : The 2012 London Olympics uniquely placed the shot put qualifiers in the British capital's iconic Greenwich Park, merging ancient with contemporary.
- **Indoor Arena** : While traditionally an outdoor sport, shot put has its indoor equivalent, allowing athletes to compete year-round. However, the Olympics maintains the outdoor tradition.
- **Close Calls** : The 1984 Olympics saw Italian Alessandro Andrei win gold by the slimmest of margins: just a single centimeter.
- **Golden Streak** : Tamara Press, representing the Soviet Union, claimed consecutive gold medals in 1960 and 1964, leaving an indelible mark on the sport.
- **Undefeated** : From 1952 to 1960, Parry O'Brien remained unbeaten in shot put, a streak that included two Olympic golds.
- **Surprising Venues** : In an attempt to make the event more spectator-friendly, the 2012 London Olympics had the qualifiers at The Mall, with Buckingham Palace as the backdrop.
- **Historic Dominance** : The U.S. men's shot putters have historically dominated, having won 18 gold medals in the Olympics since 1896.

- **Comeback King** : American Adam Nelson won silver in Sydney 2000 and Athens 2004. In 2012, he was retroactively awarded the Athens gold after the original winner was disqualified.
- **Hall of Fame** : Four-time Olympic medalist (three gold) Parry O'Brien was inducted into the U.S. Olympic Hall of Fame in 1984, cementing his status as a shot put legend.

Skeleton

- **Origins** : Skeleton racing owes its name to the bony appearance of the early sleds used. The sport's inception can be traced back to Switzerland in the late 19th century.
- **Olympic Debut** : Skeleton made its Olympic debut at the 1928 St. Moritz Games. After appearing again in 1948, it wasn't included again until the 2002 Salt Lake City Games.
- **Breakneck Speeds** : Athletes on the skeleton can reach thrilling speeds up to 130 km/h (81 mph). That's akin to freeway speeds on a tiny sled!
- **Gravity's Playground** : Athletes lie flat on their stomach, relying on minute body movements and gravity to navigate down icy tracks that can be over 1,500 meters long.
- **Heads First** : Unlike luge, where athletes go feet first, skeleton racers dive head-first, enhancing the sport's adrenaline rush.
- **Helmets** : Due to the high-risk nature of the sport, helmet designs have evolved over the years. They're uniquely crafted to withstand strong forces and protect the athlete's head.
- **Track Time** : A single skeleton run during the Olympics lasts just under a minute. However, that minute is a culmination of years of intense training.
- **Female Force** : Women's skeleton was integrated into the Olympics more recently, with the 2002 Salt Lake City Games marking their debut.

- **British Dominance** : In the 2010 Vancouver Games, British athlete Amy Williams broke the track record twice and won gold, highlighting the UK's prowess in the sport.
- **Consistency** : Latvian athlete Martins Dukurs won silver medals in 2010, 2014, and 2018, showcasing incredible consistency across three different Olympic Games.
- **Bespoke Sleds** : Athletes often have their sleds custom-made to fit their bodies perfectly. This bespoke approach ensures optimal performance and safety.
- **Artistry** : Some athletes infuse personal flair into their equipment, showcasing intricate helmet designs or uniquely decorated sleds.
- **Venue Rarity** : As of 2022, only 16 bobsleigh, luge, and skeleton tracks are recognized globally, indicating the sport's exclusivity and infrastructure demands.
- **Temperature Matters** : Track conditions change with the temperature, meaning athletes must be adept at adjusting their strategies based on the thermometer.
- **Weight Limit** : There's a maximum weight limit (sled + athlete) for competitors: 115 kg for men and 92 kg for women, ensuring a level playing field.
- **G-Force** : Athletes experience forces up to 5G, especially in curves. That's comparable to what fighter jet pilots might experience!
- **Close Finishes** : At the 2018 Pyeongchang Games, the gold and silver medalists in the women's event were separated by just 0.02 seconds, highlighting the sport's intensity.
- **Record Holder** : In 2017, Latvian Martins Dukurs set the record for most World Cup wins in men's skeleton, making him one of the sport's legends.
- **Tight Corners** : The Whistler Sliding Centre used in the 2010 Vancouver Games is known for its tight corners, especially corner 7, nicknamed "Lueders Loop."

- **Diverse Winners** : Athletes from ten different countries won medals in the skeleton at the Olympic Games between 2002 and 2018, showcasing the sport's global appeal.

Ski Jumping

- **Olympic Start** : Ski jumping began as an Olympic sport at the inaugural Winter Games in Chamonix, 1924. This competition established ski jumping as a thrilling spectator event.
- **Women's Inclusion** : Women's ski jumping made its Olympic debut quite recently at the Sochi Games in 2014, almost 90 years after the men's event was introduced.
- **Distance** : The record for the longest ski jump stands at an astonishing 253.5 meters, set by Stefan Kraft in 2017. This pushes the boundaries of human flight in sports.
- **Judging** : While distance is crucial, ski jumpers are also judged on style. This ensures that athletes aim for both reach and aesthetic appeal.
- **Hills** : There are two main hill sizes: the normal hill (K90) and the large hill (K120). The "K" denotes the hill's critical point where the slope begins to flatten.
- **Ski Design** : Athletes' skis can be a maximum of 146% of their body length. This specific proportion balances safety and aerodynamic advantages.
- **V-Style** : In the early 1990s, the V-style of jumping—where skis are spread in a V shape—became popular. It replaced the previous parallel style, offering better lift.
- **Winning Streak** : Finland's Matti Nykänen is the only ski jumper to have won all five of the sport's major events, including three Olympic golds in 1988.
- **Weather Challenges** : Ski jumping events can be significantly affected by wind conditions. This makes understanding and adjusting to wind patterns a crucial skill for competitors.

- **Inrun Speed** : Jumpers can reach speeds of up to 95 km/h on the inrun. This breakneck velocity aids their liftoff at the jump's end.
- **Safety** : Helmets became mandatory in the 2000s, a measure ensuring better safety for athletes during their daring jumps.
- **Youth Champion** : Toni Nieminen of Finland became the youngest male gold medalist at 16 years during the 1992 Albertville Games.
- **Telemark Landing** : A perfect landing in ski jumping involves the Telemark style, where one ski is placed ahead of the other in a lunge position.
- **Suit Regulations** : Athletes' suits cannot be more than 2 cm away from their body. This rule ensures that no unfair aerodynamic advantages are gained.
- **Record Holder** : Norway holds the record for the most Olympic medals in ski jumping. The country's success in the sport is historically unparalleled.
- **Team Event** : The team event was added to the Olympic program in Calgary in 1988. This meant ski jumping wasn't just an individual affair.
- **Special Jumpers** : Four athletes have managed to win the individual large hill event in two successive Olympics, showcasing consistent excellence.
- **Venue Heights** : The highest Olympic ski jump venue is at Utah Olympic Park, reaching an altitude of over 2,000 meters.
- **No Snow** : The Summer Grand Prix in ski jumping uses porcelain inruns and plastic outruns, simulating winter conditions and allowing for off-season competitions.
- **Goggles** : Ski jumpers use specialized goggles with tinted lenses to reduce glare from the snow and improve visibility during their flight.

Sled

- **Debut** : Bobsleigh made its first Olympic appearance at the inaugural Winter Games in Chamonix in 1924. This initiated the tradition of sled-based sports in the Olympics.
- **Female Pioneers** : Women's bobsleigh wasn't introduced to the Olympics until 76 years later, making its debut in the 2000 Salt Lake City Games.
- **Speed Demon** : In the luge, athletes can reach astonishing speeds of up to 140 km/h. This makes it one of the fastest non-motorized sports on land.
- **Solo Ride** : The singles luge events at the Olympics see participants lying on their back on a small sled, navigating complex tracks with mere inches between them and the icy surface.
- **Bobsleigh Weight** : The maximum weight for a two-person bobsleigh, including crew, is 390 kg for men and 340 kg for women. This ensures a combination of speed and safety.
- **Youngest Champion** : In 2014, German luger Natalie Geisenberger became the youngest Olympic champion in her sport at age 26.
- **Jamaican Surprise** : The Jamaican bobsleigh team's debut in the 1988 Calgary Games inspired the popular movie "Cool Runnings". Their participation showcased the universal appeal of the Olympics.
- **Track Length** : Olympic bobsleigh, luge, and skeleton tracks are typically between 1,200 and 1,500 meters long, requiring immense skill and precision to navigate.
- **Skeleton's Origin** : Skeleton originated in the late 1800s in Switzerland, making its Olympic debut in 1928. Remarkably, it returned as a permanent sport in 2002.
- **Luge Innovation** : Athletes use spiked gloves to grip the ice at the start of the luge, providing the initial push needed to propel themselves down the track.

- **Close Calls** : The smallest margin of victory in Olympic luge history is 0.002 seconds, recorded in 2014, emphasizing the sport's razor-thin margins.
- **Safety** : Modern sleds in all disciplines now incorporate advanced materials and designs to enhance athlete safety without compromising on speed.
- **Helmet Design** : In the skeleton, the athlete's helmets often feature intricate designs reflecting their personality or national identity.
- **Historic Tracks** : The St. Moritz-Celerina Olympic Bobrun, used in the 1928 and 1948 Olympics, is the world's only natural ice bobsleigh track still in use.
- **Team Dynamics** : Four-person bobsleigh teams require impeccable coordination, with all members synchronizing their movements for optimal speed.
- **Track Construction** : Olympic sled tracks require approximately 3,000 cubic meters of ice, equivalent to the volume of an Olympic-sized swimming pool.
- **G-Forces** : Athletes in sled disciplines can experience up to 5Gs during their descent, similar to what some fighter pilots might endure.
- **Historic Dominance** : Germany, with its legacy from both East and West Germany, has historically been a dominant force, claiming numerous medals across all sled disciplines.
- **Steering Skill** : While it appears sleds move on their own, athletes use subtle body movements to steer, making navigation an art of millimeter-perfect shifts.
- **Track Challenges** : The Olympic sled track at the Whistler Sliding Centre for the 2010 Vancouver Games was widely regarded as the world's most challenging, with 16 corners and a 152-meter vertical drop.

Snowboard

- **Inception** : Snowboarding made its official Olympic debut in the 1998 Nagano Winter Games. Before then, it was seen primarily as a rebel sport, evolving from skateboarding and surfing influences.
- **Halfpipe Origins** : The halfpipe event's inspiration comes from skateboarding. Snowboarders adapted the U-shaped skateboarding ramps to snow, creating gravity-defying aerials and tricks.
- **Parallel Giant Slalom** : This race format involves two snowboarders racing head-to-head down parallel courses. It's a blend of speed and technique, emphasizing both aspects of the sport.
- **Records** : Austria's Benjamin Karl holds the record for the most World Championship medals in parallel events, proving his consistency across multiple tournaments, including the Olympics.
- **Youngest** : In 2018, Chloe Kim, at just 17 years old, took home the gold medal in the women's halfpipe in PyeongChang, showcasing the sport's youth appeal.
- **Innovator** : Terje Håkonsen, a Norwegian snowboarder, although never an Olympian due to disagreements with the IOC format, innovated many of the tricks and styles now seen in Olympic halfpipe events.
- **Cross Racing** : The Snowboard Cross event, where four to six riders race down a course studded with jumps, berms, and obstacles, was added to the Olympic program in Turin 2006.
- **Gender Equality** : By the Sochi 2014 Winter Games, there was an equal number of men's and women's snowboarding events, underlining the Olympic movement's commitment to gender equality.
- **Big Air Debut** : The Big Air event, which involves riders launching off a massive ramp to perform tricks, was introduced in the 2018

PyeongChang Games, adding another dimension to Olympic snowboarding.

- **Global Appeal** : From 1998 to 2018, 10 different nations had won gold in snowboarding, showcasing the sport's international growth and appeal.
- **Double Gold** : In 2018, Ester Ledecká of the Czech Republic won gold in both snowboarding and Alpine skiing events, a feat never achieved before in Olympic history.
- **Freestyle Evolution** : Modern freestyle snowboarding was heavily influenced by the 1980s skateboard culture. Tricks and techniques from skate parks found their way onto the snow.
- **FIS Affiliation** : Despite its rebellious origins, snowboarding came under the jurisdiction of the International Ski Federation (FIS) in the late 1990s, a move pivotal for its Olympic inclusion.
- **Media Sensation** : The snowboarding events at the Olympics tend to draw a younger demographic, making it a valuable asset for broadcasters and advertisers targeting that age group.
- **Surprising Entries** : Countries without traditional winter sports infrastructure, like Thailand and Bermuda, have sent snowboarders to compete in the Winter Olympics.
- **No Poles** : Snowboarding evolved from an idea to create a ski-like experience without poles. Early prototypes included binding mechanisms to keep both feet on a single board.
- **Iconic Moves** : The "McTwist", an inverted aerial trick, is named after skateboarder Mike McGill. This move made its way to snowboarding and can be seen in the Olympic halfpipe events.
- **200 Runs** : For the Sochi 2014 Olympics, the Rosa Khutor Extreme Park required about 200 snowcat trips to prepare the snowboard slopes for competition.
- **Unique Boards** : Snowboards used in slalom events differ significantly from those in freestyle events, being more rigid and longer for increased speed and control.
- **Environmental Concerns** : Snowboarding's rise in popularity has brought attention to environmental issues, with many

professionals advocating for sustainable practices to combat climate change and preserve winter sports.

Soccer

- **Origins** : While soccer has been played in various forms for centuries, it officially became part of the Olympic Games in 1900. It was the first time national teams played against each other on such a grand stage.
- **Women's Inclusion** : Women's soccer made its debut at the Olympics only in 1996. Since then, it's grown in popularity and has seen some of the most iconic moments in women's sports.
- **Uruguay's Reign** : The Uruguayan national team won back-to-back Olympic golds in 1924 and 1928. These victories boosted their confidence and led them to host and win the inaugural FIFA World Cup in 1930.
- **Upsets** : Despite not being a traditional soccer powerhouse, Hungary holds the record for the most Olympic gold medals in soccer, with three victories in 1952, 1964, and 1968.
- **Age Restrictions** : To distinguish the Olympic tournament from the FIFA World Cup, since 1992, the men's competition has been an U-23 tournament. This rule brings out young talents, with the exception of three over-age players allowed per team.
- **USA Dominance** : The USA women's soccer team has won four Olympic gold medals, more than any other nation. Their intense training regimes and teamwork have set them apart on the global stage.
- **Absences** : From 1928 to 1980, the Olympic soccer tournament was not considered significant by many European and South American countries. This was due to FIFA's World Cup, which started in 1930, overshadowing it.
- **Africa's Pride** : Nigeria became the first African nation to win a gold medal in soccer during the 1996 Atlanta Games. This victory

was monumental for the African continent and soccer growth therein.

- **Iconic Venues** : The Maracanã Stadium in Rio, which hosted the 2016 Olympic soccer finals, is one of the most iconic soccer venues globally, having a seating capacity of over 78,000.
- **Surprising Entrants** : Iraq's soccer team managed to reach the semifinals in the 2004 Athens Olympics, showcasing that talent can shine regardless of the political and societal challenges back home.
- **Cold War Clash** : In 1952, during the height of the Cold War, Yugoslavia's victory over the Soviet Union in soccer was about more than just sports. It reflected deep-rooted political tensions.
- **Unbeaten Record** : Hungary has an unbeaten record of 17 matches in Olympic soccer from 1964 to 1980. A testament to their strength and consistency during that period.
- **Iconic Goals** : Abby Wambach's 122nd-minute goal in the 2011 quarter-final against Brazil is one of the most memorable moments. It helped the USA advance and showcased the magic of Olympic soccer.
- **Amateur Era** : Until 1984, only amateur players were allowed to compete in Olympic soccer. This changed as the definition of "amateurism" evolved, and professionals started to take center stage.
- **Drawn-out Match** : The longest Olympic soccer match lasted 2 hours and 43 minutes, when the Soviet Union beat Yugoslavia in 1960 after extra time. It showed the grit and determination of the players.
- **Diverse Medals** : Soccer is among the few Olympic sports where European and South American teams do not dominate entirely. Teams from Africa and North America have also clinched the gold.
- **Frequent Changes** : Over the years, Olympic soccer has seen several changes in its format, ranging from the number of teams

to the qualification processes. It reflects the sport's evolving nature and global appeal.

- **Big Scores** : The biggest margin of victory in Olympic soccer history was when Denmark defeated France 17-1 in 1908. It remains an Olympic record for the most goals scored in a single match.
- **First Red Card** : In the 1976 Montreal Olympics, Bouna Cissoko from Guinea received the first red card in Olympic soccer history. A reminder that passion can sometimes lead to unintended consequences.
- **Humble Beginnings** : The early Olympic soccer tournaments, especially the 1900 Paris Games, were informal. In fact, club teams represented some nations, showcasing the sport's amateur roots.

Swimming

- **Ancient Origins** : Swimming events have been part of the Olympic program since ancient Greece, but modern Olympic swimming races commenced in 1896 for men and in 1912 for women. Women's inclusion showcased the gradual shift towards gender equality in sports.
- **Outdoor Pools** : The 1908 London Games held swimming events in a pool built inside the running track's infield. It was a unique arrangement, blending the athletics and swimming venues.
- **Dominated Phelps** : Michael Phelps, an American swimmer, holds the record for the most Olympic gold medals by an individual athlete, amassing 23 golds from 2004 to 2016. His prowess in the pool remains unparalleled.
- **Youngest Champion** : In 1936, a 13-year-old named Marjorie Gestring won a gold medal in diving. Her age is a testament that talent knows no age limit.

- **Efficiency Matters** : At the 1988 Seoul Olympics, Anthony Nesty won the 100m butterfly by just 0.01 seconds. This highlights the significance of every millisecond in the pool.
- **First Goggles** : Swimmers at the 1976 Montreal Olympics were among the first to use goggles in competition. Before this, swimmers braved the chlorine without such protection.
- **Distance Variety** : The longest Olympic swimming race is the men's 1500m freestyle, which can take over 15 minutes to complete. Contrastingly, the shortest race, the 50m freestyle, often finishes in under 25 seconds, showcasing swimmers' versatility.
- **Dress Code** : The 2008 Beijing Olympics saw the introduction of polyurethane full-body suits, leading to numerous records. However, due to their performance-enhancing nature, they were banned the following year.
- **Pool Specifications** : Olympic swimming pools are required to be 50m long, 25m wide, and at least 2m deep, ensuring consistent conditions for competitors worldwide.
- **Heated Rivalry** : During the Cold War, intense rivalries between U.S. and Soviet swimmers often reflected geopolitical tensions. Their races were not just for medals but for national pride.
- **Stunning Debut** : The 1976 Montreal Olympics witnessed 14-year-old Nadia Comăneci score the first-ever perfect 10 in gymnastics. Her incredible feat is still talked about today.
- **Tied Gold** : At the 1984 Los Angeles Olympics, American swimmers Nancy Hogshead and Carrie Steinseifer both clocked 55.92 seconds in the 100m freestyle, resulting in a shared gold medal.
- **Underwater Prowess** : The 1988 Games saw swimmers employ an underwater dolphin kick for a significant portion of races, most notably by Michael Gross and David Berkoff. This strategy was later restricted to limit the underwater distance.
- **Synchronized Success** : Synchronized swimming, a blend of athleticism and artistry, debuted at the Olympics in 1984. Its

inclusion represented a broader definition of sport in the Olympic realm.

- **Butterfly Evolution** : The butterfly stroke was initially developed as a variant of the breaststroke before being recognized as a separate style in the 1950s. It's a reminder of how sports continually evolve.
- **Early Parity** : The 1912 Stockholm Olympics was the first where women could compete in swimming. While still limited, it was a significant step towards gender equality in sports.
- **Blindfolded Dive** : In the early 20th century, divers were sometimes blindfolded in training to ensure they relied on technique rather than sight. This quirky method was believed to refine their skills.
- **Turbulent Waters** : The 1900 Paris Olympics featured an underwater swimming event where competitors earned points for the distance and time they stayed submerged. It was a one-time event, reflecting the experimental nature of early modern Olympics.
- **Exemplary Endurance** : The marathon 10km open water swim, showcasing extreme endurance, was added to the Olympic roster in 2008. Swimmers battle not only each other but also the elements.
- **Swim Legend** : Duke Kahanamoku, a native Hawaiian, popularized surfing but was also a three-time Olympic gold medalist in swimming in the 1910s and 1920s. His athletic versatility continues to inspire.

Synchronized Swimming

- **Origins** : Synchronized swimming's Olympic journey began as a demonstration sport in the 1952 Helsinki Games. By 1984, it had secured its official spot in the Olympic program, celebrating both athleticism and artistry.

- **Men's Exclusion** : While men have been competing in synchronized swimming since the early 1940s, they have yet to compete in this event in the Olympics. The games have only hosted women's synchronized swimming events.
- **Extended Hold** : Swimmers sometimes hold their breath for up to a minute while executing intricate maneuvers. This showcases their exceptional lung capacity and training.
- **Name Evolution** : The sport was initially called 'water ballet', hinting at its origins in water pageantry and theatricality. Only later did it evolve into the competitive "synchronized swimming" we know today.
- **Innovative Nose Clips** : Swimmers use nose clips to prevent water from entering their nostrils. Though they seem small, these tools are essential for executing complex, underwater moves.
- **Music Matters** : Routines are performed to music, which is played both above and below water. This ensures swimmers can hear the rhythm, even when submerged.
- **Russia's Reign** : From 2000 to 2016, Russia won every Olympic gold medal available in synchronized swimming. Their dominance speaks volumes about the country's training and dedication to the sport.
- **Jelled Hair** : Swimmers often use gelatin to keep their hair in place during routines. This peculiar yet effective method prevents loose strands during performances.
- **Perfect Score** : At the 1992 Barcelona Olympics, the Canadian team received a perfect score of 100 for their technical routine. Such scores are exceedingly rare in the world of synchronized swimming.
- **Judging Criteria** : Scoring considers both technical merit and artistic impression, each marked out of 50 points. This balance ensures teams excel in both precision and creativity.
- **Unique Pools** : Olympic synchronized swimming pools are required to be at least 3 meters deep. This depth provides safety for swimmers as they perform acrobatic stunts.

- **Event Expansion** : Initially, only solo and duet events were included. However, the team event was added in the 1996 Atlanta Games, allowing larger squads to showcase their synchronized skills.
- **Underwater Speakers** : Introduced in the 1960s, underwater speakers transformed the sport, allowing swimmers to maintain synchronization even when submerged, further emphasizing the synergy between sport and music.
- **Weighted Costumes** : Athletes wear custom-made, weighted costumes to help them sink rapidly for certain maneuvers. Such details are crucial for impeccable performance.
- **Iconic Scene** : The film "Million Dollar Mermaid" featuring Esther Williams popularized synchronized swimming in the 1950s. Esther's routines inspired many and elevated the sport's profile.
- **Duets Return** : After a hiatus, the duet synchronized swimming event returned to the Olympics at the 1984 Los Angeles Games. Its reintroduction celebrated the sport's growing appeal.
- **Footwear** : Swimmers sometimes wear specialized shoes during practice to increase resistance, honing their strength and endurance for the main performance.
- **Pioneering Figures** : Annette Kellerman, an Australian swimmer, is credited with pioneering synchronized swimming in the early 20th century. Her innovative routines laid the foundation for modern performances.
- **Hydrodynamic Makeup** : Athletes wear waterproof makeup during routines. This ensures they look impeccable from start to finish, even after intense water immersion.
- **Discipline and Dedication** : An elite synchronized swimmer typically trains for about 8 hours a day, six days a week. Their exceptional discipline and dedication power their flawless Olympic performances.

Table Tennis

- **Debut** : Table tennis made its Olympic debut in the 1988 Seoul Games. Its inclusion added a touch of rapid reflexes and delicate spins to the Olympic sporting palette.
- **Speed** : The fastest spin ever recorded on a table tennis ball is over 9,000 revolutions per minute. This showcases the incredible skills and techniques athletes bring to the table during the games.
- **China's Dominance** : From its Olympic introduction in 1988 until 2016, China won 28 out of the possible 32 gold medals in table tennis. Their prowess in this sport is unparalleled on the Olympic stage.
- **Compactness** : Olympic table tennis balls measure precisely 40mm in diameter. Despite their small size, their journey in matches can be incredibly intense and unpredictable.
- **Evolution** : The sport was initially played using books as racquets and a golf ball. It's fascinating to consider this humble beginning in contrast to the elite Olympic competitions we see today.
- **Waldner Wizardry** : Jan-Ove Waldner of Sweden is often dubbed the "Mozart of Table Tennis." Competing in five Olympics, he remains a legendary figure in the sport.
- **Singles Inception** : The Olympics only featured team table tennis events until the 2008 Beijing Games when singles were reintroduced, allowing for more individual showcase of talent.
- **Sounds** : Players often rely on the sound of the ball's bounce to judge its spin. In the cacophony of the Olympic arena, this underlines the importance of sharp sensory skills.
- **Material Shift** : Before the 1950s, rackets were primarily wooden. The introduction of sponge rubber transformed gameplay, amplifying spins and speeds.

- **Age Wonder** : In 2012, Ariel Hsing, just 16 years old, represented the USA, highlighting that prodigious talent can emerge at a young age in table tennis.
- **Pioneering Nations** : The inaugural 1988 table tennis events were won by athletes from South Korea and China. These countries set an early standard for excellence in the sport.
- **Rally Record** : The longest recorded table tennis rally, with 8 hours and 15 minutes, occurred outside the Olympics. While not seen in the Games, it emphasizes the sport's potential for endurance.
- **Defensive Mastery** : Some Olympic players adopt a 'chopping' style, focusing on defense. This counter-intuitive approach can baffle aggressive opponents, revealing the sport's rich strategic depth.
- **Ball Color** : White and orange are the official ball colors. The choice depends on the table's color, ensuring optimum visibility during Olympic matches.
- **Serving Secrets** : Players often practice secretive serve techniques, unveiling them only at crucial Olympic moments, adding an element of surprise and strategy.
- **Height Factor** : The Olympic table stands precisely 76cm high. This standardized height ensures a level playing field for all competitors.
- **Twin Triumph** : In 2008, Chinese twins Jiang Yanjiao and Jiang Huajun both competed in table tennis, though for different teams - China and Hong Kong, respectively.
- **Continuous Play** : Since its Olympic inception, table tennis hasn't had a single year of discontinuation. It's a testament to its enduring appeal and worldwide popularity.
- **Venue Quieten** : During the 2012 London Olympics, organizers had to request the crowd to quieten down during serves. The intensity and passion for table tennis were palpable.
- **Racket Layers** : Olympic table tennis rackets have a complex layered structure, often comprising wood, carbon fiber, and

sponge. This blend ensures optimal speed, spin, and control during matches.

Taekwondo

- **Debut** : Taekwondo was introduced as a demonstration sport in the 1988 Seoul Olympics. It wasn't until the 2000 Sydney Olympics that it gained full medal status.
- **Scoring** : Unlike many martial arts, in Olympic Taekwondo, athletes can score additional points for the level of difficulty, like spinning kicks, showcasing the sport's dynamic nature.
- **Korean Roots** : Originating from Korea, Taekwondo translates to "the way of foot and fist." Its Olympic inclusion not only celebrated the sport but also its rich cultural heritage.
- **Protective Gear** : Athletes wear electronic protective gear. Sensors detect the strength and location of strikes, ensuring accurate and fair scoring during Olympic matches.
- **Categories** : There are four weight categories each for men and women in the Olympic Taekwondo events. This ensures fair competition based on an athlete's physique and strength.
- **Golden Point** : In case of a tie, a "golden point" round decides the winner. It's a tense showdown where the first to score wins, amplifying the drama in Olympic matches.
- **Age Range** : In 2016, Kimia Alizadeh Zenoorin of Iran became the youngest female Olympic medalist in Taekwondo at just 18 years. Such achievements emphasize the sport's appeal across ages.
- **Female First** : At the 2012 London Olympics, Gabon's Sarah Bouaouni became the first African woman to win a gold medal in Taekwondo, shattering continental records.
- **Pioneering Nations** : South Korea, the birthplace of Taekwondo, unsurprisingly leads the Olympic medal tally, illustrating their enduring mastery in this martial art.

- **Double Triumph** : In 2004, siblings Steven and Diana Lopez from the USA both clinched medals, showcasing that Taekwondo talent can run in families.
- **Gesture** : Athletes perform a bow before and after matches, respecting their opponents. This gesture, deeply rooted in Asian traditions, symbolizes the sport's inherent discipline.
- **Headgear Color** : In Olympic Taekwondo, one competitor wears blue headgear (Chung) and the other red (Hong). These colors help differentiate the competitors and their corresponding scoring displays.
- **Eight Techniques** : There are precisely eight key kicking techniques in Olympic Taekwondo. These techniques form the foundation of an athlete's offensive and defensive arsenal.
- **World Taekwondo** : Formerly known as the "World Taekwondo Federation," the organization changed its name in 2017. It continues to oversee the sport's Olympic representation.
- **Video Replay** : Starting 2009, a video replay system was introduced. Athletes can now challenge decisions, ensuring transparency in Olympic Taekwondo bouts.
- **Poomsae** : While not part of the Olympic format, "Poomsae" or forms, are integral to Taekwondo. They are choreographed patterns of defense-and-attack motions.
- **2020 Barrier** : In the Tokyo 2020 Olympics, Anastasia Zolotic made history by becoming the first American woman to win gold in Taekwondo.
- **Kyorugi** : The Olympic style of sparring is termed "Kyorugi." This full-contact format is a thrilling showcase of the sport's rapid kicks and punches.
- **Card System** : Referees can issue penalty cards in Olympic Taekwondo. The blue and red cards help maintain discipline and sportsmanship during intense bouts.
- **Height Factor** : Taller fighters often have a reach advantage in Taekwondo. However, at the 2012 Olympics, shorter competitors

showcased incredible agility, proving that technique can triumph over height.

Tennis

- **Comeback** : After being part of the initial modern Olympics in 1896, tennis was removed in 1924. It made its much-anticipated return in 1988, after a 64-year absence.
- **Golden Slam** : Steffi Graf remains the only tennis player to complete the Golden Slam. In 1988, she won all four major Grand Slams and the Olympic gold in Seoul.
- **Surface Shift** : The 2012 London Olympics had tennis played on grass courts at Wimbledon. Just weeks after the annual Grand Slam event, it was a rare occurrence to witness Olympic matches on this iconic surface.
- **Double Gold** : In 2012, Serena and Venus Williams became the first tennis players to win four Olympic gold medals, showcasing their dominance on the world stage.
- **Underhand Serve** : Monica Puig, who won gold in 2016 for Puerto Rico, occasionally used the unconventional underhand serve, adding a tactical twist to her matches.
- **Youngest Winner** : Jennifer Capriati was just 16 when she won gold in 1992. Her youthful exuberance and skillful gameplay thrilled audiences at the Barcelona Olympics.
- **Marathon Match** : At the 2012 Olympics, Jo-Wilfried Tsonga defeated Milos Raonic in a 3-set match lasting 3 hours and 57 minutes, the longest three-set singles in Olympic history.
- **Mixed Doubles Return** : After an absence of 88 years, mixed doubles made its comeback at the 2012 London Olympics, offering players another avenue for medals.
- **Multinational Medalists** : Players like Roger Federer (Switzerland) and Martina Hingis (Swiss) have won Olympic medals for different countries in doubles, proving tennis to be a globally unifying sport.

- **Pioneer** : Charlotte Cooper, in 1900, became the first individual female Olympic champion by winning the women's singles and mixed doubles in tennis.
- **Withdrawal** : Despite being the favorite, Rafael Nadal withdrew from the 2016 Rio Olympics due to wrist injuries, showing the physical demands of tennis.
- **Sibling Rivalry** : Serena and Venus Williams have faced each other in Olympic finals. Their sibling matches are always intense, and watching them on the Olympic stage is enthralling.
- **Winning Streak** : The USA holds the record for the most Olympic tennis medals with over 20, including both the early and modern eras of the games.
- **Age No Bar** : At the 1920 Olympics, Louis Raymond was 42 when he won his mixed doubles gold, proving age is just a number in the world of tennis.
- **Unique Courts** : For the 2016 Rio Olympics, the tennis courts were a distinctive blue, different from the traditional green, enhancing the visibility of the ball.
- **Big Four Dominance** : Novak Djokovic, Roger Federer, Rafael Nadal, and Andy Murray – known as the Big Four – all participated in the 2012 Olympics, making it one of the most competitive events.
- **Double Duty** : Some tennis players compete in both singles and doubles during the Olympics, showcasing their versatility and endurance.
- **Rise of the Underdog** : In 2004, Chile's Nicolás Massú won gold in both singles and doubles, surprising many and making it one of the memorable underdog stories.
- **Finalist Repeat** : Just weeks after the Wimbledon finals in 2012, Federer and Murray faced each other again at the same venue for the Olympic gold, with Murray emerging victorious.
- **Historic Venue** : The 2020 Tokyo Olympics tennis events were held at the Ariake Tennis Park, which can accommodate over

20,000 spectators, making it one of the grandest Olympic tennis venues.

Triathlon

- **Inception** : The triathlon made its Olympic debut quite recently in the year 2000 at the Sydney Games. Before that, despite its global popularity, it wasn't part of the Olympic events.
- **First Winners** : Switzerland's Brigitte McMahon and Canada's Simon Whitfield became the first athletes to win Olympic gold in the triathlon in Sydney 2000.
- **Distance** : An Olympic triathlon consists of a 1.5 km swim, a 40 km bike ride, and a 10 km run. These standardized distances ensure consistency across international competitions.
- **Youth Inclusion** : In 2010, the triathlon was included in the inaugural Youth Olympic Games in Singapore, highlighting its growing appeal among younger athletes.
- **Continuous Racing** : Unlike many other Olympic events, triathletes don't get any breaks. They transition immediately from swimming to cycling to running.
- **Quickest Transition** : The fastest transition from swim to bike, known as T1, was recorded at 24.08 seconds by Richard Varga in the Rio 2016 Games.
- **Tie for Gold** : In a rare event during the Tokyo 2020 Games, Georgia Taylor-Brown of Great Britain and Jessica Learmonth were awarded a tie, demonstrating just how closely contested the triathlon can be.
- **Drafting Allowed** : In the Olympic triathlon, athletes can draft behind each other during the cycling segment, a strategy not allowed in many non-Olympic triathlon events.
- **Brownlee Brothers** : The 2016 Rio Olympics saw the British Brownlee brothers, Alistair and Jonathan, secure gold and silver respectively, making them the first siblings to share the triathlon podium.

- **Unique Start** : The mass start is unique to the Olympic triathlon. Athletes dive into the water en masse, creating a thrilling spectacle for viewers.
- **Record Holder** : Alistair Brownlee holds the fastest Olympic triathlon time, completing the course in 1:45:01 during the London 2012 Games.
- **Equal Representation** : The triathlon is one of the few sports in the Olympics where men and women compete over the exact same race distance.
- **Diverse Winners** : By 2020, athletes from 7 different nations had won gold medals in the triathlon, highlighting the sport's international appeal and competitive nature.
- **Environmental Consideration** : At the Tokyo 2020 Olympics, the triathlon start time was adjusted due to anticipated high temperatures, showcasing the adaptability of the event and concern for athletes' well-being.
- **Team Relays** : Introduced in the 2020 Tokyo Olympics, the mixed relay saw teams of two men and two women from each country competing, further promoting gender equality.
- **Island Course** : In the 2004 Athens Olympics, the triathlon was held in the historic Vouliagmeni Olympic Centre, offering competitors a unique island-based course.
- **Flat Tyre Drama** : In 2012, Australian favorite Emma Moffatt suffered a flat tyre during the bike segment, highlighting the unpredictable nature of the event.
- **Qualification** : Athletes must compete in a series of International Triathlon Union races over two years to qualify for the Olympics, ensuring only the best compete.
- **Oldest Competitor** : At the age of 42, Rob Barel of the Netherlands competed in the men's triathlon at the Sydney 2000 Olympics, demonstrating that age isn't a barrier in this demanding sport.

- **Course Variability** : The triathlon is unique as the course changes with every Olympic venue, ranging from ocean swims in Rio to freshwater swims in London.

Triple Jump

- **Ancient Origins** : The triple jump has its roots in the ancient Olympic Games held in Greece. Back then, it was known as the "hop, skip, and jump."
- **Modern Introduction** : The triple jump was incorporated into the modern Olympic Games in 1896 for men. However, women had to wait until 1996 to compete in this event.
- **Consistency** : Viktor Saneyev of the Soviet Union won the men's triple jump gold in three consecutive Olympics: 1968, 1972, and 1976.
- **Record Breaker** : Jonathan Edwards from Great Britain set an Olympic record in 1996 with a jump of 18.29 meters, a record that still stands.
- **Dominant Nation** : The United States dominated the early years of the men's triple jump, winning gold in every edition from 1900 to 1928.
- **Late Introduction** : Even though men have been competing since the start, women's triple jump was only introduced to the Olympics in 1996 at the Atlanta Games.
- **First Female Gold** : In 1996, Inessa Kravets of Ukraine won the first-ever women's triple jump gold medal with a leap of 15.33 meters.
- **Yardstick** : The 18-meter mark in the men's event and the 15-meter mark in the women's event are considered elite benchmarks in Olympic triple jump competitions.
- **Venue Change** : Due to heavy rain at the 1900 Paris Olympics, the triple jump had to be moved indoors to ensure the safety of the athletes.

- **Wind Assistance** : Jumps are deemed invalid in records if there is a wind assistance of more than 2.0 m/s, ensuring fairness across all competitions.
- **Sand Factor** : The right consistency of sand in the pit is crucial. Too hard, and athletes risk injury; too soft, and it can affect the jump distance.
- **Closest Contest** : At the 2000 Sydney Olympics, Jonathan Edwards won gold by just 1 centimeter, emphasizing the fine margins of the event.
- **Hop Dominance** : The hop phase usually accounts for 50-60% of the total jump distance, making it a crucial part of the event.
- **Consistency Matters** : Francoise Mbango Etone of Cameroon won back-to-back golds in 2004 and 2008, becoming the first woman to achieve this in the triple jump.
- **Jump Sequence** : Contrary to popular belief, athletes can't just jump any way they like. The sequence must be a hop, followed by a step, and then a jump.
- **Oldest Medalist** : Adhemar da Silva of Brazil was 35 years old when he secured a bronze in the 1956 Melbourne Olympics, proving age is but a number.
- **All-time Best** : While not during the Olympics, Inessa Kravets holds the world record for the longest triple jump by a woman at 15.50 meters.
- **Multiple Talents** : Many triple jumpers also compete in the long jump. For example, Christian Taylor, a gold medalist in the triple jump, has also achieved remarkable distances in the long jump.
- **Technique Evolution** : Over the years, techniques have evolved, with athletes focusing more on speed during the run-up and using arms effectively for balance and momentum.
- **Shared Medals** : In a rare event at the 1912 Stockholm Olympics, both Georg Åberg and Erik Almlöf from Sweden were awarded silver medals in the men's triple jump.

Volleyball and Beach Volleyball

- **Inception:** Volleyball made its Olympic debut back in 1964 during the Tokyo Games. Since then, it's been a favorite among spectators. Beach volleyball, on the other hand, was introduced later in 1996 during the Atlanta Games.
- **Differences:** Though they share a name and basic rules, the number of players is different: six in volleyball and just two in beach volleyball.
- **Golden Dominance:** The Brazilian teams have been incredibly dominant in beach volleyball, securing numerous gold medals since its Olympic inception.
- **Quick Match:** The quickest match in Olympic beach volleyball history lasted only 33 minutes during the 2004 Athens Games.
- **Unique Setting:** The 2012 London Olympics had the beach volleyball games set up in an iconic location – Horse Guards Parade, with a backdrop of the London Eye.
- **Continuous Play:** Volleyball is one of the few Olympic sports where athletes play every day throughout the tournament.
- **Serve Speed:** In indoor volleyball, the fastest serve recorded at the Olympics shot at a blistering 134 km/h.
- **Snow Variation:** As of my last update in 2021, snow volleyball is pushing for inclusion in the Winter Olympics. If approved, it would make volleyball a sport represented in both Summer and Winter Games.
- **Unified Korea:** In a show of unity, North and South Korea fielded a unified women's team for the 2018 World Championships.
- **Venue Size:** The beach volleyball venue at the Rio Olympics in 2016 had a seating capacity for 12,000 spectators, making it one of the largest temporary venues in Olympic history.
- **Longest Rally:** One of the longest recorded rallies in Olympic volleyball lasted an incredible 2 minutes and 35 seconds in the 2000 Sydney Olympics.

- **Tallest Player:** Russia's Dmitriy Muserskiy, standing at 2.18 meters (7 feet 2 inches), was one of the tallest volleyball players in Olympic history when he played in 2012.
- **Shifting Sands:** The sand in beach volleyball must meet strict criteria. For the Olympics, around 3,000 tons of sand is often imported to meet these requirements.
- **Pioneering:** Karch Kiraly is the only player to have won Olympic gold in both indoor (1984 and 1988) and beach volleyball (1996).
- **Record Audience:** Beach volleyball matches during the 1996 Atlanta Games attracted over 1.5 million viewers, highlighting the sport's immense popularity.
- **Footwear:** Unlike indoor volleyball, beach volleyball players compete barefoot, making the sport a unique blend of athleticism and adaptability.
- **Comeback Kings:** At the 2000 Sydney Olympics, the Yugoslavian men's team overcame political turmoil and war back home to win gold, a testament to their resilience and skill.
- **High Jumpers:** Many volleyball players have an impressive vertical jump, with some male players reaching up to 3.65 meters and females reaching 3.15 meters in spikes.
- **First Winner:** The Soviet Union's women's team won the first-ever Olympic volleyball gold in 1964, setting a precedent for future tournaments.
- **Changing Ball:** In the 2008 Beijing Olympics, a new type of volleyball with dimples, similar to a golf ball, was introduced. It was designed to make its flight more stable.

Water Polo

- **Genesis:** Water polo found its Olympic berth in 1900, making it one of the first team sports in the Olympic program. Interestingly, it's also the oldest continual Olympic team sport.

- **Women's Inclusion:** Women had to wait until the Sydney 2000 Olympics to compete in water polo, a whole century after the men's debut.
- **Dominance:** Hungary holds the record for the most Olympic gold medals in water polo, with nine victories spanning from 1932 to 2008.
- **Chaos Match:** The 1956 Melbourne Olympics witnessed the infamous "Blood in the Water" match between Hungary and the USSR, stemming from political tensions, which had to be halted when it turned violent.
- **Duration:** An Olympic water polo match lasts for 32 minutes, but with stoppages, timeouts, and breaks, games often extend beyond an hour.
- **Caps:** Players wear caps, which are not just for protection, but they also help distinguish teams. White caps are for one team, blue for the other, and the goalkeepers wear red.
- **Ball Handling:** Players can only handle the ball with one hand at a time, except for the goalkeeper, who is allowed to use both hands.
- **Treading Water:** Athletes often tread water for the entire match, demonstrating their immense stamina. They can cover up to 3 kilometers in a single match without touching the pool bottom.
- **Hat-trick Hero:** Manuel Estiarte of Spain holds the record for playing in six Olympic tournaments from 1980 to 2000, a rare feat for any athlete.
- **Undefeated:** Between 1928 and 1952, the Hungarian team remained undefeated in Olympic play, showcasing their unparalleled dominance.
- **Draws:** Unlike many other sports, Olympic water polo matches can't end in a tie. If teams are level at full-time, they go to a penalty shootout.
- **Scoring Galore:** The highest number of goals scored by a team in an Olympic match is 31, achieved by Hungary against South Korea in 1988.

- **Endurance:** Water polo players often swim about 1.5 to 3 km during an Olympic match, proving the sport's demand for physical fitness.
- **Crowded Pool:** The 1900 Paris Olympics water polo competition was rather unusual with club teams participating, and the Osborne Swimming Club of Manchester took the gold.
- **Ejection:** Players can be temporarily ejected from the game for major fouls. If they accumulate three major fouls, they're out of the game entirely.
- **Ageless Wonders:** The oldest water polo Olympian was Hungary's Oszkár Abay-Nemes, who competed at age 41 in the 1936 Berlin Olympics.
- **Rapid Goals:** In the 2012 Olympics, Spain's Iván Pérez scored a goal just 5 seconds into the match against Kazakhstan, marking one of the fastest goals in Olympic history.
- **Indoor Shift:** Though traditionally an outdoor sport, water polo matches in the Olympics have been played indoors since the 2000 Sydney Games to avoid weather interruptions.
- **Final Match:** The final of the men's water polo at the 2004 Athens Olympics between Hungary and Serbia and Montenegro is considered one of the best matches ever, with Hungary winning its third consecutive gold.
- **Original Ball:** In its initial years, water polo was played using a leather ball. The transition to the modern rubber version made the game faster and more dynamic.

Weightlifting

- **Origins:** Weightlifting made its Olympic debut in 1896 in Athens. However, after a brief hiatus, it returned in 1920 and has been a mainstay ever since.
- **Women's Turn:** Women had to wait until the 2000 Sydney Olympics to compete in weightlifting, significantly expanding the sport's Olympic scope.

- **Dominance:** The Soviet Union has bagged a whopping 39 gold medals in weightlifting, making them the most successful nation in the sport at the Olympics.
- **One-handed Era:** In the early Olympic Games, weightlifters competed in a one-handed lift category. This quirky event was eventually replaced by the two-handed lifts we see today.
- **Young Prodigy:** At just 17 years old, Taner Sagir of Turkey became the youngest male Olympic weightlifting champion during the 2004 Athens Games.
- **Ageless Strength:** Conversely, the oldest male weightlifter to secure a gold was Austria's Josef Straßberger, aged 38, at the 1924 Paris Olympics.
- **Historic Lift:** In 1956, Paul Anderson of the USA raised 413.5 kg in the Clean and Jerk, the heaviest weight ever lifted in Olympic competition.
- **Dynamic Categories:** Over the years, the weight categories in Olympic weightlifting have been regularly changed and adjusted to ensure fairness and competitiveness.
- **Perfect Score:** Naim Süleymanoğlu of Turkey, nicknamed "Pocket Hercules", achieved a perfect score in the 1988 Seoul Olympics, breaking six world records.
- **Diverse Winners:** In the 2012 London Olympics, eight gold medals in weightlifting were awarded to athletes from eight different countries, showcasing the sport's global appeal.
- **Equipment Evolution:** Originally, weightlifting competitions used globular bells. The modern barbell design, more efficient for lifting, replaced them.
- **Doping Scandals:** The 1976 Montreal Olympics saw numerous weightlifters disqualified for anabolic steroid use, marking the Games' first major doping scandal.
- **Triple Triumph:** Only four weightlifters, including legends like Pyrros Dimas and Halil Mutlu, have secured gold at three separate Olympic Games.

- **Miraculous Comeback:** After a 64-year medal drought, the USA clinched a weightlifting medal at the 2016 Rio Olympics thanks to Sarah Robles.
- **Historic Ban:** In 2017, due to doping violations, the International Olympic Committee sanctioned the entire Bulgarian weightlifting team, barring them from the 2016 Rio Games.
- **Safety First:** The weightlifting platform in the Olympics is 4 meters by 4 meters, designed to provide a safe area for athletes to drop weights without damage.
- **Double Achievement:** Kakhi Kakhiashvili achieved a unique feat by winning gold for two different nations: Unified Team in 1992 and Greece in 1996 and 2000.
- **Record Setter:** Liao Hui of China broke three world records in the 69 kg category at the 2008 Beijing Olympics, proving his dominance.
- **Quick Lift:** The entire weightlifting process, from lifting the weight off the ground to the overhead position, typically lasts less than a second.
- **Equal Play:** The 2020 Tokyo Olympics marked a milestone as the number of weight categories for men and women was made equal for the first time.

Wrestling (Greco-Roman and Freestyle)

- **Antiquity:** Wrestling is one of the oldest Olympic sports, with its origins dating back to the Ancient Olympic Games in 708 BC. This makes it one of the few sports with millennia-long Olympic traditions.
- **Distinction:** Greco-Roman wrestling, introduced in the 1896 Olympics, prohibits holds below the waist. This rule distinguishes it from freestyle wrestling, which allows leg holds.

- **Domination:** The Soviet Union was a wrestling powerhouse, securing a staggering 62 gold medals in both wrestling disciplines combined during their Olympic participation.
- **Lone Achievement:** In 1908, the middleweight Greco-Roman wrestling category had only one competitor, Martin Klein from Estonia. He, unfortunately, had no one to compete against, making it a unique Olympic moment.
- **Marathon Match:** In 1912, the aforementioned Martin Klein wrestled Alfred Asikainen for a grueling 11 hours and 40 minutes, marking the longest Olympic wrestling match ever.
- **Women's Debut:** Women's freestyle wrestling was only introduced to the Olympic program recently in 2004 during the Athens Games, diversifying the ancient sport.
- **Clean Sweep:** At the 1952 Helsinki Olympics, Turkey made history in Greco-Roman wrestling by winning gold in all seven weight categories, a record that still stands.
- **All-round Talent:** Ivar Johansson of Sweden is a legendary figure, clinching gold in both freestyle and Greco-Roman events during the 1932 Olympics.
- **Double Gold:** Only five wrestlers have managed to win gold medals in both freestyle and Greco-Roman wrestling at a single Olympics, showcasing their unmatched versatility.
- **Stellar Record:** Russia's Aleksandr Karelin, dubbed the "Russian Bear", remained undefeated for 13 years in international Greco-Roman wrestling and secured three Olympic golds between 1988 and 2000.
- **Close Call:** Wrestling was almost removed from the Olympic program in 2013, but a global outcry from the wrestling community ensured its continued place in the Games.
- **Rapid Triumph:** Rulon Gardner's victory over Karelin in 2000 is considered one of the greatest upsets in Olympic history, as Karelin hadn't been defeated in 15 years of international competition.

- **Venue Shift:** Wrestling events for the 1932 Los Angeles Olympics were hosted at the Grand Olympic Auditorium, a venue typically used for boxing and roller derby.
- **Weighty Issues:** The weight categories in Olympic wrestling have seen frequent changes, with the 2020 Tokyo Olympics featuring six categories each for men's freestyle, women's freestyle, and Greco-Roman.
- **Distinctive Mats:** Wrestling mats at the Olympics have a diameter of 9 meters and are typically blue, distinguishing them from other combat sports.
- **Historic Hat-trick:** Japan's Saori Yoshida clinched three consecutive Olympic golds in women's freestyle wrestling from 2004 to 2012, solidifying her legendary status.
- **Twin Triumph:** Hasan and Hüseyin Özkan, Turkish twin brothers, made history by both winning gold medals in Greco-Roman wrestling during the 2000 Sydney Olympics.
- **Unyielding Spirit:** In 2012, American wrestler Jordan Burroughs, after proclaiming "I love gold" on social media, lived up to his words by winning the Olympic gold in the 74 kg freestyle category.
- **Endurance Test:** Olympic wrestling matches consist of two three-minute periods, with the physical and strategic demands often likened to "chess with muscles."
- **Global Spread:** At the 2016 Rio Olympics, 29 different countries secured medals in wrestling, highlighting the sport's universal appeal and competitiveness.

Conclusion

As the final whistle sounds and the last medal is draped, the grand narrative of the Olympic Games reaches yet another momentary pause, only to rise again with renewed vigor and spirit in another city, under a different sky. But the essence, the beating heart of this monumental event, remains unaltered – a celebration of human potential, dedication, and the quest for excellence.

Throughout the pages of "1000 Facts about the Olympic Games", we've journeyed together through time and across continents, unearthing stories that define the very fabric of the Olympics. We've encountered tales of unsung heroes, marveled at records that seemed superhuman, and chuckled at the quirks and peculiarities that have shaped the Games. Each fact, each narrative, serves as a testament to the multifaceted nature of this event that transcends borders, politics, and prejudices.

The Olympic Games are more than just a sporting event. They are a testament to the indomitable spirit of humanity. A space where dreams are realized, where the impossible is challenged, and where unity and camaraderie overshadow differences.

In the end, the Olympic Games serve as a poignant reminder of our shared humanity and potential. Here's to the past legends, the present champions, and the future hopefuls. May the Olympic spirit continue to inspire, unite, and captivate us all.

Daniel Scott

Printed in Great Britain
by Amazon

35483305R00059